Bono

Rock Star Activist

Martha P. Trachtenberg

Enslow Publishers, Inc.
40 Industrial Road
Box 398
Berkeley Heights, NJ 07922
USA
http://www.enslow.com

Dedication

This book is dedicated to the men who rock my world, my husband and son,
Thomas and Michael Griffith.

Acknowledgments

I wish to thank the reference librarians at the South Huntington, New York, public library for their boundless enthusiasm and aid as I dove into the research for this book. My mother and first music teacher, Frances Shabshelowitz Trachtenberg, was a great source of help and encouragement, as always. I am particularly grateful for the generous assistance of Diane Lesniewski of the Harborfields library. She is a U2 fan of many years and gave me access to her private archive of articles and overseas publications.

Library of Congress Cataloging-in-Publication Data

Trachtenberg, Martha P.
    Bono: rock star activist / Martha P. Trachtenberg.
      p. cm.—(People to know today)
    Summary: "A biography of U2 lead singer Bono"—Provided by publisher.
    Includes bibliographical references and index.
    ISBN-13: 978-0-7660-2695-7
    ISBN-10: 0-7660-2695-7
    1. Bono, 1960—Juvenile literature. 2. Rock musicians—Biography—Juvenile literature. 3. U2 (Musical group)—Juvenile literature. I. Title.
    ML3930.B592T73 2008
    782.42166092—dc22
    [B]

2007016129

Printed in the United States of America
112009 Lake Book Manufacturing, Inc., Melrose Park, IL

10 9 8 7 6 5 4 3 2

To Our Readers: We have done our best to make sure all Internet addresses in this book were active and appropriate when we went to press. However, the author and publisher have no control over and assume no liability for the material available on those Internet sites or on other Web sites they may link to. Any comments or suggestions can be sent by e-mail to comments@enslow.com or to the address on the back cover.

Photos and Illustrations: AP/Wide World Photos, pp. 75, 79, 86, 88, 90, 103, 106; Serena Campanini/Rex Features, courtesy Everett Collection, p. 32; Chris Enns, p. 102; Janine Lavallée, p. 65; William Murphy, p. 9; Paramount Pictures/courtesy Everett Collection, p. 54; Brian Rasic/Rex Features, courtesy Everett Collection, p. 61; Rex Features, courtesy Everett Collection, p. 44; Phil Romans, p. 17; Mark G. Servidio, p. 4; Richard Young/Rex Features, courtesy Everett Collection, p. 96.

Cover Illustration: PA/Topham/The Image Works.

CONTENTS

1

A LOVE BEYOND FAITH

By December 2005, Bono was accustomed to seeing himself on the covers of magazines. He and his bandmates in U2 had been featured in *Rolling Stone*, *People*, and *Time*, among others. But this magazine cover was out of the ordinary, even for him. He had been named Person of the Year, along with Bill and Melinda Gates, by *Time* magazine. Billionaire Bill Gates was one of the founders of Microsoft, the computer software company. He and his wife Melinda were being honored for their charitable foundation, which has given millions of dollars to help the needy around the world. Bono was being singled out for his humanitarian work on behalf of the poor and people with AIDS. The boy from Dublin was front and center on the world stage.

It was a vastly different world from the one his parents had inhabited after World War II. Brendan

The Catholic and Protestant Conflict in Ireland

In Ireland, the differences between the two main branches of Christianity, Catholicism and Protestantism, are magnified by a political element dating back to the sixteenth century, when the English rulers tried to impose Protestantism on the largely Catholic population. After centuries of struggle for "home rule" (the control of Ireland by the Irish, not the English), which included a series of armed and bloody rebellions, six counties were politically split from the rest of the country by England and became the Protestant-dominated Northern Ireland in 1920. Northern Ireland continued to be controlled by England, while the rest of Ireland became the Irish Free State, later the Republic of Ireland, in 1922. It is only recently that all the centuries of conflict were put to an end.

Robert Hewson, known as Bobby, and Iris Elizabeth Rankin lived around the corner from one another in Dublin, and they met and fell in love when they were nineteen.[1]

They had a major obstacle to overcome before they could begin a life together, however. Bobby was a Catholic and Iris was a Protestant. The division between the two religions was deep and affected everything in daily life—you lived in a Catholic or Protestant neighborhood, and as a child, you attended a Catholic or Protestant school. It was very difficult for a Catholic and a Protestant to get married in a religious ceremony at all. A Catholic who wanted to enter into a mixed marriage had to send a petition to the Pope in Rome, seeking permission to wed a non-Catholic. The non-Catholic partner was urged to convert, to take classes on Catholicism, and was instructed to sign an oath that his or her children would be raised as Catholics. If the marriage went forward, it would be in a darkened church with no flowers or decorations to show the Church's disapproval.

Bobby thought long and hard about it, and finally decided that he wanted his and Iris's wedding day to be joyful. On August 6, 1950, he and Iris were wed in a Protestant church, in a Protestant ceremony. It was a brave step for both of them, and it was a true sign of their love for one another. Years later, a Catholic priest blessed the marriage.[2]

The newlyweds rented a place for a while, and then bought their first house. It was in Stillorgan, six miles from Dublin. Bobby worked in the post office, and Iris was a skilled homemaker. Two years after their wedding, they had their first son, Norman. On May 10, 1960, when Norman was seven, he was presented with a little brother, Paul David Hewson . . . better known today as Bono.

2

A CONFLICTED CHILD

S oon after Paul was born, his mother and her sister Ruth took him out for a stroll in his carriage. As they walked, they passed some houses that were being built in an area called Ballymun. It was close to Ruth's home, and Iris thought it would be wonderful to live nearer to her. She took the idea to Bobby, and one week later, they bought a house there.[1]

Their new home rang with the sound of Paul's crying. No matter what Iris did, the baby cried for most of the day. She brought him to a doctor, hoping he could discover the cause and a cure. No luck; Paul was healthy, and had a healthy set of lungs that he continued to exercise.[2] The doctors did suspect it had something to do with his heart, and as an adult, Bono went to a doctor who examined him and told him that he was healthy, but that he had "an eccentric heart." Bono agreed.[3]

Eventually, the crying stopped, to be replaced by speech. Paul had begun to talk—to his parents, to himself, and sometimes to more unusual listeners. When he was three years old, his father saw him poking into a bush in the backyard. He realized that a bee was on Paul's hand and called to his son, afraid that the boy would be stung. Paul's response? "No, it's all right, Dad. I've made friends with him."[4] He seemed to have made friends with a number of bees, as he was seen picking them up and chatting with them on other occasions and never was stung![5]

Bono's current home is in Killiney, a town on the outskirts of Dublin, Ireland. Bono's bandmate The Edge also lives in this exclusive residential area.

Ballymun was a mixed neighborhood, both economically and religiously. A few years after the Hewson family moved in, large apartment towers that were mostly inhabited by lower-income families replaced the fields and trees near their home.[6] The Hewson family fell more into the middle class. They owned a house and a car, and Iris was able to be a full-time homemaker, a role she enjoyed greatly.[7] Still, young Paul was not completely at ease. He found it hard to decide if he was more a part of the working class, like his neighbors in the towers, or the middle class, like his neighbors on Cedarwood Road.

Another source of discomfort was religion. Ballymun was mostly Catholic, with a smaller Protestant population. Paul was the child of a Catholic and a Protestant, and that was unusual at the time. He felt caught between the two religions. On Sunday mornings, his father would drop him, his mother, and his brother off at a Protestant church while his father waited outside.[8] He did not really know whether to call himself a Catholic or a Protestant, and when he was asked about it as an adult, he said, "I always felt like I was sitting on the fence."[9]

One of Paul's best friends at the time was a neighbor named Derek Rowen. Derek was one of eleven children, and Paul enjoyed visiting his house. The two boys shared a dislike of soccer, called football in Ireland, and discovered they both liked to draw. They spent many hours together, painting, drawing, or just going on long walks. The Rowen family also provided Paul's introduction to the idea that the Protestant and Catholic churches were not the only religious paths available. They belonged to the Plymouth Brethren, a small religious group that believed that the Bible alone was all that was required as a guide for the faithful. The Brethren rejected all the religious rituals and arguments over how God should be worshipped, and Paul found it fascinating. It was the first time he considered looking outside of the established churches but far from the last.[10]

Religion was not confined to what church he went to. It also affected what school he attended. He and his brother Norman rode a bus to the Protestant-run Glasnevin National Primary School in Dublin instead of going to the Catholic school that was in Ballymun.[11]

Paul was a bright boy who was not very interested in school. Despite that, he was at the top of his class until he switched schools at age eleven.[12] He went to St. Patrick's Secondary School for Boys and had a rough time adjusting to it. In fact, he later said he spent quite a bit of the 1971–1972 school year skipping school altogether.[13] Instead of going to classes, he would walk around the center of Dublin.

Something had to change. And in September 1972, something did.

3

HIGH SCHOOL HEAVEN

In the summer of 1972, a new school caught the attention of the press and of Bobby Hewson. Mount Temple High School was making headlines as the first nondenominational, coeducational (boys and girls) secondary school in Dublin. This meant that the student body was made up of Protestants and Catholics, with no religious slant to what was taught and no built-in separations between students from a wide variety of backgrounds. It was a great place for a child who walked the line between the two faiths and two classes.

Sure enough, Mount Temple proved to be the perfect fit for Paul. They had a casual dress code, rather than requiring a school uniform, something that Paul had always disliked.[1] The code was a reflection of their greater acceptance of individuality. It was a place where Paul could be himself, and the self that emerged was smart, talented, and popular.[2]

Paul began to play chess, and at the age of twelve, he played in an international competition. He did not win, but, he said, "I did okay. And people made a fuss over me being a kid playing against adults."[3] When he became interested in music, though, chess quickly took a backseat.

Things were going well at school. Paul's teachers enjoyed having him in class, and he was especially good in history, English, and art. He made new friends and was enjoying exploring the worlds of drama and music. At one point, he opened up his own dance club, called The Web, in a closed-down schoolhouse at Mount Temple. He was both host and DJ.[4] It was a place for him to perform, especially for the girls. He gave himself a nickname, the Spider,

Irish Education

Irish children must attend school from ages six through fifteen. The schools are separated into levels. The first level is primary school, which goes for six years, with an additional two years of kindergarten available but not mandatory. There are three different types of second-level schools, which students attend for five to six years.

Secondary school is roughly the same as American high school.

Vocational school is geared to training students for different careers.

Community and Comprehensive schools offer academic and technical classes. When students complete their second-level education, they take examinations to get a Leaving Certificate, which is similar to a high school diploma in America.

and told the girls that came to the club that he considered them to be the flies.[5]

At home, Paul was closer to his mother, Iris, than to his father. He often fought with his brother, Norman, and later took the blame for most of the arguments they had.[6] He also argued fiercely with his father, and sometimes the fights would last for hours. Mick Wall tells a story of one such scene in his book, *Bono: In the Name of Love*. Paul and his father started a war of wills after dinner one night and neither one would back down. The scene ended after two in the morning, when Paul gave in and said he was wrong. But the following morning, he marched into the kitchen and said, "I only agreed because I wanted to go to bed."[7]

Still, Bobby Hewson had faith in his difficult son. It was just a matter of getting through his teens. At least the boy was doing better at school. Things were going reasonably well on Cedarwood Road, until the unthinkable happened on September 10, 1974.

4

TRAGEDY STRIKES

Iris Rankin Hewson was the oldest of eight children,[1] and in early September 1974, her parents celebrated their fiftieth wedding anniversary with a big celebration. The entire family enjoyed a night of dinner and dancing. Her father died the next day. It was completely unexpected. His sudden death was a terrible shock to Iris, and she collapsed at his funeral while on her way back to the car with Bobby and Ruth. They rushed her to the hospital.

After four days spent in a coma, Iris died of a brain hemorrhage on September 10, 1974. Paul was only fourteen, and he was shattered. In part, he was crushed because, although his mother had been his ally in the house,[2] he felt that he had not had the chance to get to truly *know* her. Now he had forever lost the chance to do that. "There was the feeling of the house being pulled down on top of me because after the death of my mother it was not a home."[3]

For a while, he was adrift. Home had changed forever, and he needed something to take its place, something to ease his pain. He looked back as an adult and said, "The death of my mother really affected my confidence. . . . I felt abandoned, afraid. I guess fear converts to anger pretty quickly. It's still with me."[4] His loss surfaced in the lyrics to some of his songs, including "I Will Follow" and "With or Without You." Two years passed before he really found his footing again. He went back to spending time with his old friends, the Rowen family. It was a safe place for him, a source of comfort, as was the home of his long-time friend Fionan Hanvey (also known as Gavin Friday).[5]

He also found comfort, and a challenge, in a new relationship. Paul had noticed another Mount Temple student, a girl named Alison Stewart, some time before. She was beautiful, smart, and independent. She had noticed Paul, too, but she had seen for herself that he seemed to go from girlfriend to girlfriend, and she had no desire to add her name to the list. It took some time for Paul to get her to go out with him, but at the age of seventeen, they started a partnership that has grown steadily ever since.

Other friends from school, plus Paul's neighborhood pals, came together in 1977, forming a group that called itself Lypton Village. Members of the Village chose nicknames for themselves and for one another. Derek Rowen became Guggi. Fionan Hanvey became Gavin Friday. Other members of the Village were dubbed Strongman, Pompous Holmes, and Bad Dog. Paul, at Guggi's suggestion, became Bono Vox at first. The name, which means "good voice" in Latin, was spotted on a sign at a hearing aid store in Dublin. Eventually, it was shortened to Bono.[6]

The Village was into what was called "performance art"—they would put on spontaneous shows in the streets of Dublin. "We were this gang of *nut cases*. We'd get electric drills, a saw, a hose, a sweeping brush, and

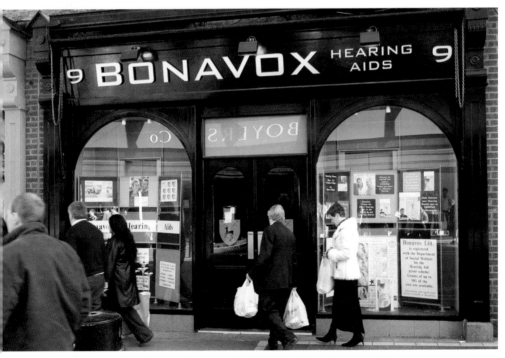

The Bonavox hearing aid store in Dublin that inspired Bono's name.

just go into the heart of the city, in the street and put on a performance. Just make it up on the spot."[7] They were united in mocking "the adult world and agreed we would never grow up because all we saw was silliness."[8]

Back at home, life had to go on, and after Iris's death, Bobby had set about making sure that the household tasks were taken care of. He made a schedule for himself, Bono, and Norman, but Bono did not always do the work assigned to him. To make matters worse, he would often have his Village friends over to the house and then fail to clean up after them.

Sometimes Bono's father would give him money to buy dinner for the family, only to find that he had spent it for something else entirely.[9] Years later, Bono recalled "I even went as far as robbing groceries from the shops, and giving the money I was given by my father for groceries to my friends."[10]

One day, Bono heard about a note that had been posted on a bulletin board by another Mount Temple student, Larry Mullen. Larry wanted to start a band and was looking for other musicians. Bono decided to give it a try.

5

A ROCK STAR IS BORN

Bono liked music, especially the punk rock that was becoming popular at the time. His brother, Norman, had taught him to play some chords on the guitar, and he had always enjoyed listening to music. Still, when he went to Larry Mullen's house, it was not because of a burning ambition to enter the music world. If anything, he was more interested in drama at the time. He and Larry were both in for a surprise.

"Bono arrived, and he meant to play the guitar, but he couldn't play very well, so he started to sing. He couldn't do that either. But he was such a charismatic character that he was in the band anyway, as soon as he arrived. I was in charge for the first five minutes, but as soon as Bono got there, I was out of a job."[1]

Finally, a band dubbed "Feedback" was put together.

It consisted of Dave "The Edge" Evans on lead guitar, his brother Dick on rhythm guitar, Adam Clayton on bass, Larry on drums, and Bono doing vocals and acting as the front man for the group. All of them went to Mount Temple and they sometimes rehearsed there.[2]

None of the members of the band were great players. They all learned as they went along. Writer Bill Flanagan described it this way in an article for *The Rolling Stone Illustrated History of Rock & Roll:* "The members of U2 are smart, and as they learned their instruments and practiced together they were bound to get better. But luck plays a part in success, too, and it was astonishingly lucky for the novice group that, as Bono got used to singing, he uncorked a terrific voice."[3]

As all this was happening, Bono was still in school at Mount Temple. He did well enough in his final year there to be able to apply for a place at University College Dublin. Although Bobby was not sure that Bono would really devote himself to schoolwork, he felt that it was only fair to let him try. He offered his son a deal. Bono could go to college for one year with his father paying all the expenses. If all went well, he could stay in school. If he goofed off, he would have to go get a job. Bono agreed, and started college in September 1977.

He was only two weeks into his classes when his father got a call from the university, saying that an error had been made in admitting him at all. Bono had failed his final exam in Irish, and he had to leave the university. Even though Irish was not a subject required for the arts degree Bono had in mind, the university refused to let him stay without going back to Mount Temple and passing that one course. Bobby Hewson was understandably enraged, but there was nothing he could do, and Bono went back to Mount Temple. He was only taking one class, so he had plenty of time to give to the band.

They rehearsed steadily and began to get gigs at local pubs and clubs, learning how to play their instruments, how to work together, and how to please a crowd. In March 1978, they entered a local talent contest and won, despite competing against bands with much more experience. The official prize was five hundred pounds (about one thousand dollars), but the real prize was that one of the judges was an executive at CBS Records, and he was so impressed by them that he took the band into the studio to record a demo. "Demo" is short for demonstration, and it was customary for bands to record a few songs—usually three—to demonstrate their sound for record companies.

In the end, the demo did not turn out too well; the band was new to recording studio work, which is a far cry from live performance, and had much to learn. Still, it was a valuable experience for them, and a confirmation that they were a cut above the other local bands.

After the band won the competition, Dick Evans left to study engineering at Dublin's Trinity College. By that time, the band had changed its name to the Hype, and they finally settled on the name U2 in 1978.[4]

The four friends took the band seriously. The more they played, the more their quartet developed its own sound and style. The band continued to work whenever and wherever they could, with their friends often coming to support them. One night, the audience included Bill Graham, a writer for *Hot Press*, an Irish rock magazine. He wound up interviewing the band, describing them as promising. He also brought them to the attention of the man who would play a major role in taking the band to the next level and then some: Paul McGuinness.

6

A "BABY BAND" TAKES
ITS FIRST STEPS

Paul McGuinness had already put in some time in the entertainment industry, and had managed one fairly successful band. He and journalist Bill Graham would talk about the music business for hours, and Paul developed his own ideas of how to turn a local band into something far greater. He told Bill that what he needed was a talented, young group that was dedicated to succeeding in the business and willing to wait for that success; it was not going to happen overnight. He wanted a "baby band." When Bill called about U2, he said that he thought he had found what Paul was looking for.[1]

McGuinness knew about the band already because Adam Clayton had been calling him and trying to get him interested in them for quite some time. The manager would put him off, and Adam would call again. And again. And again. Between Adam's persistence and Bill's recommendation, McGuinness finally decided to take a look for himself.

On May 25, 1978, he went to hear U2 play at the Project Arts Centre in Dublin. He liked what he heard and saw. "Edge's playing was quite unique. And Bono, he just looked the audience in the eyes as if to say, 'I dare you to look back.' And all I had ever seen before were performers who looked out over the audience at some imaginary spot. There was something special about them."[2]

After the concert was over, he met with the band to talk. He told them that he wanted them to think about going for long-term success, and that it would not come quickly or easily. He wanted to know if they were willing to be patient and put in the time and work that were necessary. They were, after all, just teenagers. They were committed teenagers, though, and they convinced him that they understood what he was telling them, and that they wanted to go for it.[3] By the end of that meeting, he was their manager.

His first goal was to get them on the path to a recording contract. The band needed a good demo tape, and that became the immediate goal. They spent much of that summer rehearsing for their next trip into the recording studio. They were all done with school, and they often worked on their music from morning to night.[4] In the course of spending all that time together, they developed the working relationship that was to keep them together through decades of ups and downs. They each contributed to the songs and to the sound.

Advice From the Pros:
How to Become a Music Manager

If you would rather be the person behind the scenes, managing the band itself, what will you need to know? Professional manager Mark Spector can tell you. (Interview conducted by author via email, May 2006.)

Do you recommend going to a business school or taking specific courses to prepare for managing an artist?
MS: Any relevant education can only help, whether it be a traditional business education or a "music business" program, which many schools offer these days.

What are the responsibilities of a manager?
MS: The manager is the artist's advocate and he/she is responsible for advocating in a wide variety of arenas and with a plethora of individuals. The manager must be able to see the big picture of an artist's career and be fluent in the many different aspects that will present themselves along the way. He/she must learn the responsibilities of all concerned with the artist's career in order to steer those same people toward a goal that he/she and artist have set for themselves.

What kind of income can a beginner expect?
MS: Little or none unless he gets lucky very quickly.

What kind of hours should they be prepared to put in?
MS: Long ones.

How should they pick an artist to manage?
MS: Trust your instincts.

Now based in New York City, Mark Spector has been in the music business for almost forty years and has managed many successful, respected artists, including Joan Baez, .38 Special, Patty Smyth, James McMurtry, and Mary Gauthier.

The usual sequence for local bands was to record an album and play the best local clubs. That was it. With very, very rare exceptions, the bands would settle for making good money at those clubs and go no further professionally. McGuinness had no intention of letting his "baby band" stay in the nursery. He wanted them to literally get out of town and not settle for just being a big deal in Dublin. He wanted them to invest in good equipment, both a decent sound system and a van to travel in. Most of all, he wanted them to develop a long-term relationship with a record company, a company that would support them in the studio and on the road. As he had told them that night at the club, he was looking at the big picture. The band practiced, composed, and performed through the summer. That November, they went into the studio to record three songs, with Barry Devlin as their producer. Devlin, a musician himself who was with a very successful Irish band called Horslips, was impressed. When McGuinness asked his opinion at the end of one day of recording, Devlin replied, "They are self-assured, intelligent, and funny. You will certainly have a major British success with them. It's about chemistry, Paul, and they have it."[5]

McGuinness took the new demo to record labels in London. The band had lots of good press clippings, but no labels were interested. He spent months taking it around, trying to get appointments, and traveling back and forth between Dublin and London. By March 1979, McGuinness settled for the best deal he could get, with CBS Records' Ireland branch. It was limited—the band would record a three-song album, and it would only be released in Britain.

The album was called *U2–3*, and Jackie Hayden, the CBS executive who had signed the band, came up with some wonderful marketing ideas. He went to a popular Dublin disc jockey, Dave Fanning, and convinced him to play all three songs on his show repeatedly. Fanning would then ask his listeners to vote for their favorite song, and that song would become the "A side" of the record. Keep in mind that at that time, there were no CDs. Music was released on records, and one side was marked A, the other marked B. Record labels would pick the song they thought had the best chance of success and put it on the A side so the disc jockeys would know which song to air.

Fanning's listeners picked a song called "Out of Control." So far, so good, but Hayden went one step farther. CBS had printed one thousand copies of the record, and he hand-numbered every single one of them. He figured, rightly, that it would make the records seem that much more special to the buyers, and the record stores agreed with him. It took him only two days to place all one thousand copies in stores![6]

The single made it onto the charts, and the band had their first success. But it still was not enough to get another record deal. McGuinness arranged a tour for the band that included some top clubs in London. He was sure that he could get representatives from the London-based record labels to come to their concerts, and he was also sure that hearing the band play live would do the trick. It would be an expensive trip, though. Half of the money they needed—for food, gas, equipment, and places to stay—was going to be provided by an English publishing company. The day before they were to start the tour, the band got a stunning call. The publishing company had decided they would only give the band half as much money as they had promised. In short order, the band members went to their parents and friends, and almost all of them came through with loans. The tour was on.[7] Some of the shows went well, some poorly, but none of them had the desired result of getting the band signed by a major label. They went back to Dublin and regrouped, finally deciding that they would do a tour where they were already well known and had a good audience: Ireland. They took a big gamble and ended that tour by playing in the National Boxing Stadium, a two-thousand-seat stadium in Dublin. They managed to fill one thousand of those seats, and finally succeeded in getting the attention of Bill Stewart, an A&R (artists and repertoire) man who represented Island Records.[8]

U2 had a record deal at last.

7

SUCCESS AT LAST

The first record U2 produced for Island Records was called *Boy*. It was released in October 1980 and was very well received. *Boy* was voted Best Album, Best Debut Album, and Best Album Sleeve in the *Hot Press* Irish National Poll Results.

In his review, *Rolling Stone* writer James Henke wrote, "The title *Boy* is appropriate and significant: not only are the band members young—Bono and Adam are twenty, Larry and Edge nineteen—but the bulk of their songs deal with the dreams and frustrations of childhood."[1] Jon Pareles, also writing for *Rolling Stone*, said, "*Boy* was an intriguing, one-time-only document—the inside story from children at the brink of manhood."[2] Bono later described *Boy* as "a retrospective of U2 over two years—the end of our adolescence . . ."[3]

The band went off to play their first tour of America, and it proved to be a great success. They often had the difficult job of being the "warm-up" act for better-known groups, but they managed to win over audience after audience. Ultimately, one million copies of *Boy* were sold in the United States, making it a "platinum" record.

The touring took a toll on the band, though. They were away from their families for months at a time, they were getting tired physically, and their personal differences were magnified because they were together so much.

A major issue was that three band members—Bono, Edge, and Larry Mullen—were deeply religious. They did not follow the teachings of the Catholic or Protestant churches, instead choosing to describe themselves simply as Christians, and had joined a Charismatic Christian group called Shalom. They studied the Bible and often discussed it, sitting in the back of the tour bus. They rejected the usual trappings of the rock 'n' roll lifestyle—sex, drugs, and alcohol. Bass player Adam Clayton, however, did not share their faith and was inclined to enjoy a more typical rocker's life.

Bono has since said that there came a point in 1981 when the band almost broke up.[4] In fact, Bono,

Edge, and Larry Mullen went to Paul McGuinness to tell him that they were going to call it quits, just before they were about to go out on tour for their next album, *October*, which was released in October 1982.

McGuinness talked them out of it by appealing to their sense of honor. He pointed out that they were not the only people to be considered in this decision, that it would seriously affect everyone who worked with them. By then, the band toured with crews of support people. They had all committed to spending months on the road with U2. The band had an obligation to their record company, to the promoters who were already hard at work, and to the owners of the concert venues who had booked them and could not replace them on short notice. How would letting all these people down be consistent with their Christian ideals? McGuinness did not mention the effect their decision would have on him or on Adam Clayton; it was obvious.[5]

After much soul searching, the band decided they would do their best to combine the faith so important to three of them with the music they all loved to play. They had already been successful by being true to themselves. It was now a matter of continuing to make conscious choices of how to live and what kind of message they wanted to send in their music.

October was, overall, a deeply spiritual album, and one that reflected what was going on in the band members' lives. The song "With a Shout (Jerusalem)" begins

Bono and his wife Alison Stewart in 2003.

with the lyrics, "Oh, where do we go,/Where do we go from here?" In "Rejoice," Bono sounds a theme that would be played out in his life thereafter: "I can't change the world/But I can change the world in me/Rejoice./Rejoice."

Another lifelong theme made an appearance on *October*. According to Bono, "'Tomorrow' was unconscious rambling. Years later, I realized it was a narrative account of my mother's funeral."[6]

Bono later told writer Mick Wall, "Many people found *October* hard to accept at first."[7] Still, the album got good reviews in the press, and the band added to its growing ranks of fans as they toured.

U2 was a successful band, but they were hardly rich. All the members still lived at home with their parents. Instead of Ferraris, they were driving used cars. They were holding to Paul McGuinness's plan of investing in themselves. When they toured, they would take the profits and put them into buying new equipment and hiring the best staff they could find to run it. That meant that the next tour would be even better than the last. They would sell more records and gain more fans. The band took the long view, as they had promised McGuinness back in 1978.[8] In Bono's case, taking the long view had extra meaning. On August 21,1982, he and Alison Stewart got married. Adam Clayton was Bono's best man. After eighteen months of tension on and off the road, regarding the difference in their beliefs, it was still Clayton that Bono reached out to for this special day. Edge, Larry Mullen, and other members of Shalom also participated in the ceremony.

Slowly but surely, he was finding the balance he sought between what he saw as his commitment to Christian values and his commitment to U2 and its music.

It was time for another album, and this one would once again be a mirror for the band, reflecting the issues they were concerned with at the time. *War* was released in March 1983. In June of that year, Bono said:

More than any other record, War *is right for its time. It is a slap in the face against the snap, crackle and pop. Everyone else is getting more and more style-orientated, more and more slick. John Lennon [of the Beatles] was right about that kind of music; he called it 'wallpaper music.' Very pretty, very well designed, music to eat your breakfast to. Music can be more. Its possibilities are great. Music has changed me. It has the ability to change a genera-tion. Look at what happened with Vietnam. Music changed a whole generation's attitude towards war.*[9]

He was referring to the youthful peace movement that arose in response to the war in Vietnam and to the important role that music played in that movement.

As usual, the band took risks. One song in partic-ular, "Sunday Bloody Sunday," almost did not make it onto the record. The title referred to a devastating day in 1972, when British troops in Derry, Northern Ireland, shot at unarmed Catholic demonstrators who were calling for Northern Ireland's independence from the United Kingdom. Thirteen people died, and the entire country was in an uproar. Eleven years later, "Bloody Sunday" was still a rallying cry for many. The Edge started the song, and the entire band contributed to it.[10] Rather than simply siding with the Irish against the English, or with Catholics against Protestants, they condemned the acts of violence committed by all sides. When the band went to play it out for the first time, at a club in Belfast, which is in Northern Ireland, Bono told the crowd of three thousand that if they did not like the song, U2 would never play it again. It met with a roar of approval.[11]

After the album's release, the band was interviewed for a leading British music publication, *New Music Express*. The writer remarked that *War* actually held out some hope, instead of being completely grim. Bono replied, "You have to have hope . . . I don't like music unless it has a healing effect . . . I want people to leave our concerts feeling positive, a bit more free." He added, "The album is about the struggle for love, not about war in the negative sense. . . . The power of love is always more striking when set against realism than when set against escapism."[12]

War was, by many accounts, the album that finally established U2 as a top act. A reviewer for the London magazine *Time Out* called it "a bid for massive commercial success," and described it as "marvelous."[13] It hit No. 1 on the British charts within a week of being released.[14] When the band toured in Britain, all twenty-seven of their concerts were sold out. U2 then toured America, where the album went to No. 12 on the charts. They were the headliners at last, and played to arenas that were filled with up to ten thousand fans at a time.

8

"THE BAND OF THE '80s"

Even when the *War* tour was finished, it was not exactly over. Several live recordings made during the tour were combined to create an EP titled *Under a Blood Red Sky*. "EP" is the abbreviation for "Extended Play," which is a recording that has more songs on it than a single, but fewer than are on an album. The phrase "blood red sky" was a quote from the lyrics of one of the songs on *War*, "New Year's Day."

The video that accompanied the album was filmed at an open-air concert at the Red Rocks Amphitheatre outside of Denver, Colorado, on June 5, 1983. Thousands of fans turned out despite the threat of a storm, and it proved to be an incredible show. The background consisted of stunning, enormous rock formations, and the stage was framed by large flaming torches. Today it is unthinkable for a band to release a CD without at least a couple of videos to accompany it, but videos were relatively uncommon in 1983. MTV was only two years old, and each individual video got more airtime and attention than they might today, and had greater impact on the overall scene. Years later, in 1999, *Entertainment Weekly* listed the Red Rocks concert as number forty in their 100 Greatest Moments in Rock.[1]

Rolling Stone also singled it out in their 2004 special issue, "50 Moments That Changed the History of Rock and Roll": "The sight of Bono singing the anti-violence anthem 'Sunday Bloody Sunday' while waving a white flag through crimson mist (created by a combination of wet weather, hot lights, and the illumination of those crags) became the defining image of U2's warrior-rock spirit and—shown in heavy rotation on MTV—broke the band nationwide."[2]

The album was a hit. In the *Hot Press* reader's poll, it was the No. 1 Best Album. It peaked at No. 2 on the United Kingdom album charts and made it up to No. 23 on the American album charts. *Under A Blood Red Sky* finally went multi-platinum, with three million copies sold.[3] The video was also a bestseller.

Bono and U2 were on a roll. But they knew it was time to start thinking about their next record, while they were riding the wave of acclaim the *War* tour had created. *October* had been different from *Boy*, and *War*

Advice From the Pros: How to Become a Recording Engineer or Producer

You have seen them in countless movies and music videos—recording studios equipped with tons of gear and vast control boards being run by engineers and producers. How can you become one of them? Here is some advice from award-winning engineer and producer Bil VornDick. (Interview conducted by author via email, May 2006.)

What advice would you give a kid who is interested in becoming a recording engineer or producer? Should she/he take classes at a college or tech school, or just try to get a low-level job at a studio and work up to a seat at the board?
BV: For the music business in general, get a four-year degree in Music Business. I would recommend Belmont University in Nashville, Tennessee. You can become an artist, manager, agent, public relations person, producer, recording engineer, music publisher, songwriter, concert promoter, roadie, road manager, A&R (artists and repertoire) director for a record label, and more. You can do sound recording and forensics for the CIA or FBI; be a sound engineer for concerts; do sound for the White House, television stations, foreign embassies, and the armed forces; or get into record promotion, tour support, and advertising. The entertainment business is the largest business in the world.

What kind of life can a recording engineer expect? Is it a nine-to-five job or a steady diet of all-nighters?
BV: My life in production is normally fourteen-hour days. When I started, I was working eighteen hours a day. They need to love what they do.

What is the income level for beginners?
BV: Better than McDonald's, but they will have to work hard and prove themselves.

Are there Web sites you'd recommend?
BV: Try www.Belmont.edu for Belmont University and www.aesnashville.org or www.aes.org for the Audio Engineering Society.

Any extra advice?
BV: Make sure you use earplugs when you go to a concert or ride on a subway. Keep your headphones at a lower level while listening to your CD player or iPod. Never put your window all of the way down when you ride in a car – the wind's low frequencies can ruin your hearing.
Grammy Award–winning producer and engineer Bil VornDick has been in the studio as a sound engineer and/or producer for artists such as Bob Dylan, Bela Fleck, Dolly Parton, and James Taylor.

different from *October*. As Eamon Dunphy put it in *Unforgettable Fire*, "They didn't want their next album to be *Son of War*."[4] What would they do this time?

For openers, the band decided to work with a different producer. Steve Lillywhite had produced their first three records, and Jimmy Iovine was credited as the producer for *Blood Red Sky*. This time, U2 turned to Brian Eno, who had started out as a successful musician and then moved into producing. Eno invited Canadian engineer Daniel Lanois to come along with him.

The title of the album came from something the band had seen at Chicago's Peace Museum. It was a collection of paintings and drawings created by survivors of the bombing of Hiroshima and Nagasaki in World War II. In addition to that exhibition, the museum had a section dedicated to Martin Luther King Jr. and the civil rights movement.

The band left the museum inspired and moved, and those images and emotions provided the basis for the songs that would be written for *The Unforgettable Fire*. It was not an easy process, though. The writing went very slowly, they were in awe of Eno, and they began to wonder if they could get what was in their heads and hearts onto tape.[5]

Years later, Bono was asked about the album, and replied, "We knew there was a more experimental side that was important. Enter Brian Eno and Danny

Lanois. Even when the lyrics weren't strong, the subject matter was. So now the music starts catching up with the subject matter and beautiful sonic landscapes. The guitar playing starts to get very otherworldly."[6]

"'Pride' started out as an ecstatic rant. We looked for a subject big enough to demand this level of emotion that was coming out. We had discovered non-violence and Martin Luther King, not just in relation to his use of the Scriptures and his church background, but also as a solution to the Irish problems."[7]

The album was released in October 1984 to mixed reviews, but it still went to the top of the charts, hitting No. 1 in Britain and No. 12 in America. "Pride" became U2's first song to hit America's Top 40. As usual, the band went out on tour to support the album, traveling first to Australia and New Zealand, then back to Europe, and finally to the United States.

U2 decided to give all the money from the American tour to Amnesty International, a group that seeks to protect human rights all around the globe. The band chose to use its popularity and drawing power to assist causes it supported, and it was just the beginning.

By the spring of 1985, U2 was on the cover of *Rolling Stone,* under the headline "The Band of the '80s."[8] And the decade was not even half over.

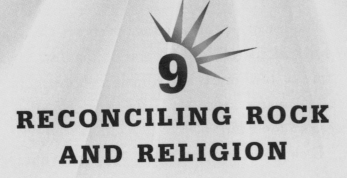

9

RECONCILING ROCK AND RELIGION

In early 1985, Bob Geldof was hitting the phones. Geldof, a member of the successful Irish band The Boomtown Rats, was trying to organize two major concerts that would take place on the same day, July 13, 1985. One was in Wembley Stadium in London, England. The other in JFK Stadium in Philadelphia, Pennsylvania. Both programs were broadcast live around the world, with pleas for listeners to donate money.

Previously, Geldof had organized a large number of musicians—including Bono—under the name Band Aid to make a fund-raising record for those dying of famine in Africa. Band Aid released the song "Do They Know It's Christmas?" in December 1984 and it went on to become one of the best-selling singles of the year. Now, Geldof's two-city concert project would be called Live Aid.

The list of performers for the shows was a who's who of rock 'n' roll, and U2 was on that list. It was to be one of their most memorable performances, and one that many critics have said truly cemented their place as a top band.

Each group was given fifteen to twenty minutes to perform.[1] U2 planned to do three songs. They started their set with "Sunday Bloody Sunday" and then began "Bad," a song from *The Unforgettable Fire*. The band was going to end the set with "Pride (In the Name of Love)," which was getting lots of airplay at the time. They never made it there. First, Bono began to improvise, as he often did at U2 concerts, throwing in pieces of other songs. Then he decided that he wanted to reach out to the audience, as usual, but a large pit in front of the stage and lots of security people made it very slow going. He finally reached his goal and pulled a young woman out to dance with him. When he was done, there was no time left for the third song.

Bono was crushed. "This was a big show for our band, there were a billion people watching, and we didn't do our big song. Everyone was very annoyed with me, I mean, *very* annoyed. . . . It ruined my day. I thought I'd ruined the band's performance."[2] But his decision to venture into the crowd, to make contact, was proved right in the following days. People flooded into record stores "asking for something by 'the singer that danced with the girl at Live Aid.'"[3] The feedback was overwhelmingly positive, and what could have been a massive mistake became one of the most talked-about highlights of the entire concert.

Live Aid was aired in 150 countries and eventually raised $140 million.[4] Bono said:

> For Bob Geldof, the sight of little bits of black plastic [records, tapes] actually saving lives was something of a shock. He had always thought of pop music as something wonderful in itself, but nothing more. I wasn't quite as taken aback by the success of it all. The '60s music that inspired me eventually helped to stop the Vietnam war, and there is no reason why contemporary music cannot have a similar importance. I've always believed that music could help to change things, not in any melodramatic way, but certainly as part of a movement of positive protest. There are new problems and we need new solutions.[5]

Bono wanted to be part of the solution. After the show, he told his wife Alison, "I just can't get these people I'm seeing on television out of my head. We have to try and do something. In a quiet way."[6] They went to work in a refugee camp in Ethiopia for one month, and they did go quietly. The press only found out about it toward the end of their stay; they were not there to get publicity. While they were at the camp, Bono and Ali

U2's performance at 1985's Live Aid is seen as one of their best moments on stage by both fans and critics.

worked with the staff at an orphanage, writing plays and educational songs that were about "the things they needed to know in order to not be sick. So I wrote songs and they were translated into Amharic . . . . The children would then go around, singing these songs and so teach their parents." At the time, Bono had especially long hair and wore earrings, and was dubbed "The Girl with the Beard."[7]

He had gone to Ethiopia in part because he worried that the growing success of U2 was separating him from his religious principles. After the trip, he refused to talk much about what he had done, wanting the spotlight to be on the famine in Africa, not on him. He did say, though, "I got more than I gave to Ethiopia."[8] Three years later, photographs of their time in Africa were displayed in Dublin. The exhibition was titled *A String of Pearls* and was later published as a book with the same name.

Bono was back on the road with the band in 1986. U2 was one of several groups touring the United States on behalf of Amnesty International. By the time the tour was over, Amnesty International's American membership had doubled.[9] In July 1986, the band also played a benefit for their countrymen in Ireland. The show was called Self Aid, and raised half a million pounds (approximately one million dollars) to help the unemployed.

Bono also participated in a recording project for Artists United Against Apartheid, a group of musicians organized by musician Steven van Zandt to protest the existence of apartheid in South Africa. "Apartheid" means racial segregation. In South Africa, apartheid was a policy used by the ruling white minority to keep the black majority impoverished and powerless. They released a single called "Sun City," named after a lavish, whites-only resort in South Africa that became a symbol for apartheid, and followed it up with an album of the same name. Bono contributed a song called "Silver and Gold" and recorded it with the help of Keith Richards and Ron Wood of the Rolling Stones. It was later recorded by U2 and chosen as the B-side of their single "Where the Streets Have No Name."[10]

Bono's determination to combine his Christian ethics and beliefs with rock 'n' roll was as strong as ever. In the course of a couple of years, he had used his position as a celebrity to benefit Amnesty International, Live Aid and the famine victims in Africa, the unemployed in Ireland, and Artists United Against Apartheid. But when all was said and done, his ability to do good for all these organizations stemmed from his career as a musician, and it was once again time to go back to the studio.

10

"THE BIG ONE"

The Joshua tree is a tall, hardy cactus that grows in the Mojave Desert in the southwestern United States. It is said that the name came from Mormon pioneers who thought that the uplifted, bent arms of the cactus resembled the prophet Joshua, urging them to move forward to the promised land.

When Steve Pond reviewed U2's *The Joshua Tree* album for *Rolling Stone* in April 1987, he wrote, "The title befits a record that concerns itself with resilience in the face of utter social and political desolation, a record steeped in religious imagery." He also said that *The Joshua Tree* "could be the big one" for U2.[1]

He was absolutely right. And he was not the only one who felt that way. Music critics were almost unanimous in praising the album. On April 27, 1987, U2 became the third musical group to be on the cover of *Time* magazine, joining the Beatles and the Who. The cover story was titled "U2: Rock's Hottest Ticket." They were.

Hit single followed hit single—"Where the Streets Have No Name," "With or Without You," and "I Still Haven't Found What I'm Looking For" kept U2 on the radio for months. Bono and his bandmates managed to combine irresistible music with lyrics that dealt with deep, sometimes grim, subject matter. Their second collaboration with producers Daniel Lanois and Brian Eno paid off with an album that proved to be their biggest seller yet, and Bono gave the producers credit for pointing the band in new directions. "I think when Eno and Lanois came in, they made us look at other music like gospel and soul, they helped us develop an atmosphere, develop our songs. I think *The Unforgettable Fire* is where we found our feet and *The Joshua Tree* is where we start to walk, to maybe even run."[2]

The Joshua Tree started at No. 7 on the American album charts and moved up to No. 1 three weeks later. It was the first U2 album to reach the top of the charts in the United States and it was an international bestseller as well, reaching the No. 1 spot in the United Kingdom, Canada, West Germany, the Netherlands, Australia, and Switzerland. By the end of 1987, *The*

Joshua Tree had been certified as platinum (million-seller) four times over.

When the Grammy Awards ceremony honoring 1987 releases was held in March 1988, it was no surprise when U2 walked away with Album of the Year and Best Rock Performance by a Duo or Group with Vocal. They were also nominated in the categories of Record of the Year and Song of the Year.

The songs on *The Joshua Tree* touched on topics that were important to the band, including spirituality, relationships, conflicts in South and Central America, drug abuse, and, to their sorrow, the death of a dear friend. "One Tree Hill" was written as a memorial to Greg Carroll, a crewmember from New Zealand who died in a motorcycle accident while running an errand for Bono.

As usual, the band toured after the record's release, and this time they had 110 concerts scheduled in America, Canada, and Europe. The tour would keep them on the road for more than a year.[3] This time, they were playing in sold-out stadiums and arenas, and whether they liked it or not, they had entered the world of big business. Their fans loved them as the lads from Dublin, but the lads had to accept that they had gone from being musical underdogs to being one of the top bands in the world.

All the acclaim meant that the members of the band found themselves in the media spotlight, on and off stage, far more than ever before. Bono, as the front man for the group, was often singled out for extra attention, and that took some getting used to, despite the fact that he had been performing for so many years. He talked about it with one of his idols, American songwriting legend Bob Dylan:

> *It was at the height of* Joshua Tree *madness. We were on the cover of* Time *magazine, and we had number-one singles, albums. It was very, very exciting, but a head trip too. There was a lot coming at us, just disorienting stuff. And he [Dylan] said, 'Imagine going through all that you're going through, now, on your own.' I can't imagine what it would be not to have . . . Edge or Larry to speak [to] through the side of my mouth about something ridiculous, and laugh to ourselves.*[4]

Still, they were stars, and they all had to come to grips with it. Bono told one interviewer, "I don't feel like a pop star, and I don't think I look like one." When pushed to talk about his goals, now that he was a star, he said, "To inspire people to do things for themselves. To inspire people to think for themselves. . . . We are in a big sleep, where I'm okay, you're okay. And we don't ask questions that have difficult answers. And if U2 is throwing cold water over that kind of thinking and people are waking—that's fine."[5]

Bono had some hard thinking of his own to do. Life on the road was good for record sales, but tough on his marriage. "I hardly saw Ali, my wife, for a year. Nineteen eighty-six was an incredibly bad year for me. It's almost impossible to be married and be in a band on the road—but Ali is able to make it work. Then you tell the press that she is her own person and very smart . . . and they read into it a marital breakdown."[6]

What is more, he and Ali were starting to think about having children, and while Bono was sure that Ali would be a wonderful mother, he did not have nearly as much faith in himself. "I'm both frightened and excited by it. I feel just too irresponsible. The kid would end up being my father. I'm the sort of guy where the son is sent out to fetch his dad and bring him home. But I think Ali would be an amazing mother, and it might be exciting to see new life. I'd just be afraid that if it were a boy, it would turn out like me."[7]

Bono was a work in progress:

Since I was seventeen I've been in this band and it so happens that most of my friends are musicians or writers, what have you. Now all my identity has been wrapped up in this life, this U2 thing. Recently, I've got to thinking this isn't such a healthy thing. In all other areas I'm a total embarrassment. Socially, God, I'm a social inept. That's what makes me laugh when people ask me what it's like being a rock 'n' roll star. I'm the last person to ask. I have no understanding of that.[8]

He was honing his skills as a singer and developing his craft as a songwriter:

There's a discipline, a tradition of directness in popular songwriting that I'm only starting to come to terms with. Take Van Morrison: he started off singing songs about girls—"Gloria" and stuff. Then fifteen years later, he came up against the spiritual higher ground—[his album] Inarticulate Speech of the Heart. *Me, I got it all back to front! I started with the spiritual stuff, now I'm learning to write songs about girls.*[9]

At the same time, Bono was learning about issues such as poverty, AIDS, apartheid, and political oppression that would lead him into greater and greater involvement with people and groups who were seeking solutions. He did not know then that years later, he would go from assisting in others' humanitarian campaigns to launching a few of his own.

11

MEDIA FRENZY AND SOCIAL CHANGE

Several concerts from The *Joshua Tree* tour were filmed, and a combination of those performances and new studio recordings was released in October 1988 as a movie, a double album, and an accompanying book, all entitled *Rattle and Hum*. Bono said the movie was "about myself, Adam, Edge, and Larry—three men and a baby."[1]

The music chosen reflected the band's fascination with American roots music—early rock 'n' roll, rhythm and blues, country, gospel, and blues. It was also a mix of U2 songs and covers of songs written by others, including the Beatles and Bob Dylan. A reviewer for the English music publication, *New Music Express*, called it "a messy if immensely intriguing album" and "an odd beast."[2] The record was a hit, reaching the No. 1 spot in England and in America, but overall the project met with less success than *The Joshua Tree*.

By the end of The *Joshua Tree* tour, Bono told a visiting journalist, "It seemed for a time that everybody wanted a piece of us. They wanted to put U2 on their walls like a plaque—businessmen and politicians who hadn't even heard a song. . . . It all gets too absurd . . . . We're on the run from the politicians and the TV crews and all the people who think they own a piece of U2. We're gonna lock the doors, make music and keep them out."[3]

(left to right) The Edge, Bono, Larry Mullen Jr., and Adam Clayton in 1988's *Rattle and Hum*.

Once the band was finally off the road, Bono did just that. He went home, took the phone off the hook, refused to do interviews, and started working on lyrics for new songs.[4] He also had to start working on his parenting skills. His first child was born on his twenty-ninth birthday, May 10, 1989, and he and Ali named their daughter Jordan.

Later that year, the band was on the road again. This tour was dubbed The Lovetown Tour, and was split into two parts. From September through December 1, 1989, they toured in New Zealand, Australia, and Japan. They had nine whole days off, during which time everything (and everyone) had to be shipped halfway around the world, and picked up again in France, Germany, Holland, and Ireland. They skipped America, where they had reached the point of being overexposed. Between the *Joshua Tree* album and tour, the *Rattle and Hum* album, movie, and book, and press coverage of the band's political and social activism, the press had had enough of U2 for a while.

Even the band members had had their fill; as Edge told one reporter, "I'm sick to death of reading about U2." Bono added, "There is a sense of 'Up drawbridge,' cut ourselves off, and a sense of feeling misunderstood, and a sense of the antagonism toward us." He went on to say that the band had been advised not to release another record anytime soon because it would not sell too well. "But so what? We don't have to do anything we don't want to do now. That is what it is to be rich—and in that sense, we are *filthy* rich. We used to have to finish albums and go on tour just to stay solvent, right up until *The Joshua Tree*. We don't have to do that now, so we're just gonna play where we want to play."[5]

On New Year's Eve, 1989, U2 played at The Point Depot in Dublin, and the show was televised internationally. Bono sparked fears that the band was breaking up when he stood onstage and said that it was "time to go away and dream it all up again."[6]

In fact, there was a three-year gap between the release of *Rattle and Hum* and the next U2 album, *Achtung Baby*. During that time, they hardly dropped off the press's radar, even if there were fewer front-page articles. Two of their albums were featured in *Rolling Stone*'s list of the best one hundred albums of the eighties: *The Joshua Tree* was No. 3 and *War* was No. 40.[7] U2 won the Best International Group prize at the Brit Awards in London in February 1990.[8] The next month, Bono was picked as Sexiest Male Rock Artist and Best Songwriter in a *Rolling Stone* readers' poll. The band was still on *Rolling Stone*'s readers' minds in 1991, when another readers' poll put U2 into fourth place in the Best Band category.

Bono had another reason to celebrate during that period. July of 1991 saw the birth of his and Ali's second daughter, Memphis Eve.

In October 1990, the band went to Berlin to start work on their next album project. They were meeting with producers Brian Eno and Daniel Lanois. Bono wanted to be in Berlin at that time because great changes were in the air, revolutionary changes, and he thought it was the right place for U2 to be, for inspiration.

The Berlin Wall had divided the city since the end of World War II and was the physical symbol of the way Germany had been split in half by the war's victors. West Berlin had a democratic government and East Berlin was controlled by Communist Russia. The Wall had been torn down in November 1989, and West and East Germany were finally being officially reunified when U2 arrived in Berlin in October 1990. It seemed that the entire city was out in the streets to mark the event, and the band set out to be a part of the celebration. Sure enough, they found a parade and joined it. But after a short time, they realized that their fellow marchers were not filled with joy by the collapse of the Wall; they found they were walking with people protesting the changes![9]

When they made it into the studio, they found the going was tough there, too. U2 had a major choice to make. Should they stick with the sound and instrumentation that had brought them such success, or should they keep pushing the boundaries and experiment with new sounds, new technology? Bono and Edge wanted to explore, and Clayton and Mullen wanted to keep their original sound.

The band members disagreed so strongly that they began to seriously question whether they should stay together. Fortunately, Brian Eno was able to step in and show them that they were not nearly as far apart as they thought. Daniel Lanois later commented, "If you manage to get the four of them in one room with instruments in their hands you're going to get results. That has a lot to do with my job—just getting them in the room and playing."[10] They played. The turning point came when Edge began to work out a new riff and the rest of the band joined in. In the course of that day and night, the song "One" was written, a song that would later be hailed as one of the ten most influential records of all time.[11] The storm had passed, and they were sailing again.

In November 1991, *Achtung Baby* hit the record stores, and in February 1992, U2 hit the road.

12

LIFE IN A ZOO

*A*chtung means "Attention" in German, and the public certainly paid attention to U2's newest release. *Achtung Baby* marched right to the top of the charts, reaching No. 1 in the United Kingdom and No. 2 in the United States. As usual, the album went multi-platinum, with tremendous international sales.[1]

In the end, Bono and Edge had succeeded in getting Adam Clayton and Larry Mullen to try newer sounds, and the subject matter had shifted as well. The band was entering its second decade and the band members were entering their third, and the record reflected it. "*Achtung Baby* implied that as U2 hit their thirties they were inclined to get into the sort of mischief they had missed by spending their late teens and twenties concerned with grave matters of sin and salvation. The album was about both the fun of sneaking out for a wild

Saturday night and the guilt and hangover of Sunday morning."[2]

Their sound was not the only thing they chose to update. When the band went out on tour in February 1992, audiences were faced with a radically different show than they had come to expect. The tour was dubbed Zoo TV, and a zoo it was—an expensive zoo. Bono later admitted:

> *We were risking bankruptcy. You see, Zoo TV cost so much . . . it cost a quarter of a million dollars a day to take that thing around. So, if ten percent less people had come to see us, we'd have gone bankrupt, and with those kinds of bills, you don't go bankrupt a little, you go bankrupt a lot. . . . I remember speaking to Ali about the consequences of failure. She was fearless: 'What's the worst, to sell the house, and get a smaller one . . . What's wrong with that?' . . . That's the only time I actually thought about failure. I never thought about it up to that.[3]*

The reason for the high cost of the show was plainly visible on the stage. It was decked with TV sets and video screens, all displaying a stream of constantly changing images, and all requiring a small army of support people. There were rotating mirrors, flashing

Bono performs as Mister MacPhisto at Wembley Stadium in London in 1993.

lights, and a lead singer who sounded like Bono, but had a radically different look. Several of them, in fact.

Bono had consulted with Fintan Fitzgerald, the band's stylist, and the two of them altered his appearance in several ways. His shoulder-length brown hair was now short and black, and for his first stage outfit he sported a pair of bubble-eye wraparound sunglasses and a skintight leather suit. When he dressed this way, he was called The Fly. The Fly was followed by Mirrorball Man, for which Bono wore a suit covered in small mirrors and stood before a full-length mirror admiring himself. This character was a "glittering tribute to televangelists all over the world."[4] Finally, Bono returned to the stage in a gold lamé suit, looking like a combination of the devil and Elvis, and going by the name Mister MacPhisto.

When he talked about the show later, Bono explained that he had chosen to take on some of the different sides of himself that had been criticized in the press—the egotistical rock star charmer (The Fly), the Christian preacher (Mirrorball Man), and the aging but devilish rock god (MacPhisto).[5] He poked fun at himself and had a ball. In one interview, he talked about how a friend had asked him how his ego survived his being a star. "I thought that was one of the smartest things anyone had ever spotted about rock 'n' roll. People think it's the opposite, that it pumps up your ego. I think it explodes your ego. It blows it out into fragments . . . . So what U2 decided to do, with *Achtung Baby!* and the tour, is to explode our egos—publicly."[6]

It was a stunning show and it played to sold-out stadiums in the United States, Canada, Mexico, and Europe from February to November 1992. Bono pulled quite a few pranks onstage, including calling a pizzeria and ordering ten thousand pizzas for the fans, and calling the White House and asking to speak to President Bush.

When the band got home, they were still jazzed from the high energy of the show and the tour. They had four months off between the first leg of the tour and the second, which was to be in Europe. Instead of taking a well-earned break, they produced another album in only six weeks, this one entitled *Zooropa*. It included a guest vocalist for the first time, country star Johnny Cash. He sang the last song on the album, "The Wanderer." The Edge also did a lead vocal. Bass player Adam Clayton later remarked, "I think *Zooropa* achieves a new language for Bono to use—a language that's more his own, that he feels more comfortable with."[7]

In May 1993, the band returned to the road. The tour was now entitled Zooropa, and they played in Europe for three months. They rested for three months and polished off the tour with a couple of months in Australia, New Zealand, and Japan, this time calling it

Advice From the Pros:
How to Become a Sound Technician

If you are interested in a career working with sound equipment, what do you need to learn now? Experienced sound technician David Schnirman has been there, done that, and can tell you all about it. (Interview conducted by author via email, May 2006.)

How can a kid prepare for a career as a sound technician?
DS: If they want to be a tech (someone who prepares audio equipment for use/sets it up/repairs it), they can begin by unplugging the audio equipment in their home and putting it back together. [Author's Note: Please clear this with your parents first!] A basic knowledge of electronics and physics will be very useful.

An audio engineer "mixes" sound. Mixing is the process of taking individual inputs/instrument sounds (snare drum, violin, piano, guitar, bass, or vocals, for example) and blending them together into a pleasant sound. If they want to be an audio engineer who mixes the sound for live shows, they need to:

1. Listen to a great deal of music and discover how the sounds they are listening to are put together. Why is one sound in the foreground while others are further back in the mix, etc.

2. Listen to the instruments. When played live, how do they produce the sound? Are they plucked, hit with sticks, hammers, bowed, etc.? What do they sound like acoustically?

3. Learn to play an instrument or sing.

4. Study what sound equipment is used for. How does combining the different elements (microphones, processors, amplifiers, speakers) create the sound you desire?
Should he/she go to college or a tech school?
DS: If the person wants to just plug things together and learn to do repairs, a tech school is good.

If you want to take it further, mix sound/design systems/do sound design for theater, then college is a good starting point, and not because you will come out knowing everything you need. College will open you up to many different audio experiences—theater, music, film, dance, lectures, radio, television, recording, producing, etc.

I suggest that once you have a focus and graduate, you intern for a company that does that type of work. The best way to learn is by doing it.

Everyone starts from the ground up; no one jumps right in at the top. In order to be good at what you do, you have to practice your skills, study the history of the field you are in, and stay aware of the trends, of where things are going.
Should they simply attach themselves to a band or a company like yours and learn as they go?

Zoomerang. Surely two albums and months of touring would be more than enough to fill up anyone's schedule, but Bono found time for a few side projects in those years. He wrote songs for two films directed by Wim Wenders, *Until the End of the World* in 1991 and *Faraway, So Close!* in 1993. In 1992, he and the Edge bought the Clarence Hotel, a seventy-bedroom hotel in Dublin. They had it converted into a five-star, forty-nine-bedroom hotel that "quickly gained a reputation as one of the most stylish (and expensive) hotels in the city."[8]

The Clarence Hotel in Dublin, Ireland.

In 1993, Bono recorded a track for Frank Sinatra's *Duets* album. He had had visions of meeting and singing with the legendary crooner, but he wound up recording his part of the song in Ireland and sending it off to America to be mixed in. A year later, Bono paid tribute to Sinatra at the Grammys, where he was being honored with a lifetime achievement award. Also in 1993, Bono and his old friends Gavin Friday and Maurice Seezer cowrote two songs for the soundtrack of a film set in Ireland, *In the Name of the Father.*[9]

The *Zooropa* album had been something of a musical experiment for U2, and it was well-received. As usual, it reached the No. 1 spot on the charts internationally, and went multi-platinum. In 1994, it won a Grammy Award for Best Alternative Music Album. U2 would not release another album until 1997.

That did not mean that they were not in the studio, though. In 1995, they released a single, "Hold Me Thrill Me Kiss Me Kill Me," which was the theme song for the film *Batman Forever*. It was the biggest hit they had had in Britain since "The Fly" reached No. 2 in the summer of 1991.

The next project was one that Bono was pushing for strongly. It was a collection of musical pieces, both long and short, titled *Original Soundtracks 1*. He drew his inspiration from a variety of film clips and images and worked closely with the Edge and producer Brian

Eno. The song that became a hit, "Miss Sarajevo," was accompanied by footage of the war in Bosnia. It was a duet between Bono and the internationally famed operatic tenor Luciano Pavarotti. U2 played the music, and Bono wanted this project to be their next album, but the record company pointed out that it really was not in keeping with U2's body of work. Moreover, the single was connected with a documentary film about the siege of Sarajevo, which was also titled *Miss Sarajevo*. Bono was the executive producer of the film, which won several awards. He ultimately agreed with the record company's point of view, and in the album's credits, U2 became the Passengers. It was hardly a secret that the Passengers were really U2, but the name did the job of making it clear that this was not an official U2 release. The record reached No. 12 in Britain and No. 76 in America.[10]

In January 1996, U2 got back to work in earnest. They went into the studio in Dublin and began to put their next album together. It was a convenient setup for them, as they could stay in their own homes while they developed the ideas and sounds they wanted. They worked this way for three months and then headed overseas to South Beach Studios in Miami, Florida. There they explored new musical possibilities, including working with a successful disc jockey named DJ Howie B. Howie had been a part of the *Original Soundtracks 1* project, and he brought a whole new world of music with him, including acid jazz, trip-hop, and techno. The band was interested in the sounds that were being heard in dance clubs, rather than the standard rock that was being played on the radio. They brought in Nellee Hooper, who had coproduced "Hold Me Thrill Me Kiss Me Kill Me" with Bono and The Edge, and who also knew his way around the newest techno-pop and electronic sounds.[11]

The resulting album, *Pop*, was released in February 1997. It was the first U2 album since *Zooropa* in 1993, and U2's fans could not buy it fast enough. Despite a mixed response from the critics, *Pop* popped up to the top of the charts around the world.

Naturally, they had to go back on the road, and this time they had to come up with a stage show that would be at least as exciting as the Zoo TV show had been. The result was dubbed PopMart. Afterward, Bono said, "I can't quite remember how we got the idea of taking a supermarket on the road. But I remember it made a lot of sense at the time."[12] It was not your everyday supermarket, of course. The props included an enormous television screen (170 by 56 feet), a hundred-foot Golden Arch, and a twelve-foot stuffed olive complete with a hundred-foot-long toothpick. Perhaps the wildest piece was a huge lemon covered with mirrors. The lemon would open up to let the band spring out onto the stage. Except for one night, when it stayed resolutely shut.

The band was playing in Oslo, Norway, on August 6, 1997. They were inside the lemon, waiting to emerge and play an encore, when something went wrong. Their manager, Paul McGuinness, was watching from the wings. Sometime later, an interviewer asked him what had gone through his mind when the lemon failed to open:

Utter panic. But also a feeling of immense relief that it was not me inside. I was standing there as it opened. It did open about a foot and I could see the eight feet of my clients but not the rest of them. As I watched, they tried to close it first and open it again and it was well and truly jammed. It then made a retreat to its starting position and they had to climb out the back and out to the B stage. I really felt for them.[13]

Lemon aside, the tour was a success. PopMart was the second-highest grossing tour of 1997, earning just under $80 million. One night in particular stood out.

It was their show in Sarajevo on September 23, 1997, where U2 was the first major group to play a concert after the end of the war in Bosnia. It was an exceptional event. "For two magical hours, the Irish rock band U2 and its slashing brand of rock 'n' roll achieved what warriors, politicians and diplomats have so far been unable to do: unite Bosnia."[14] About forty-five thousand people went to the concert, crossing all the barriers that had divided them for so long. Earlier that day, the band met the new Bosnian president, Alija Izetbegovic. Bono said that U2's message was "a simple one: that music is beyond politics." It was that night.

The PopMart tour ultimately lasted for almost a year with occasional breaks. It started in North America in April 1997 and ended in South Africa in March 1998. On the night of the last show of the tour, Bono told the Johannesburg audience, "To be united— to be 'One'—is a great thing. But to be tolerant, to respect differences may be even a greater thing."[15] PopMart made stops in the United Kingdom, Europe, Asia, South America, Australia, and New Zealand. In the process, U2 played to more than two million people.

Did they go home and take a break after all that?

Of course not.

13
WORKING TOWARD A BETTER WORLD

ono's comment before the Sarajevo concert—"music is beyond politics"—was a message he and the band later brought to Belfast, Northern Ireland. They visited Belfast on May 19, 1998, to perform a concert in support of the historic Good Friday Peace Agreement, which brought an end to more than thirty years of violence in Northern Ireland.[1] Bono later called that concert "the greatest honor of my life in Ireland. . . . We got John Hume and David Trimble, the two opposing leaders in the conflict, to shake hands onstage. . . . People tell me that rock concert and that staged photograph pushed the people into ratifying the peace agreement. I'd like to think that's true."[2] What added an extra edge to the show was that the band, and Bono in particular, had gotten death threats in the past for criticizing the actions of the Irish Republican Army (IRA). Playing in Belfast was not the safest choice for them, but it proved to be a good one. The band returned on August 26 and played to forty thousand fans, shortly after the agreement was voted into law and the IRA agreed to a ceasefire. One of the officers in charge of security for the August event was stunned by the behavior of the fans, saying, "Crowds make me nervous but this one doesn't. Everyone is in agreement for a change. It's quite extraordinary."[3]

Later that year, John Hume and David Trimble won the Nobel Peace Prize for their work on the peace agreement, and Bono hosted a dinner for Hume and his wife. A video of Bono congratulating the two men was aired during the ceremony in Oslo when Hume and Trimble were given their prize. In years to come, Bono would find himself being nominated for the Nobel Peace Prize.

In the meantime, he returned to the humanitarian work that was so important to him. He started by appearing in Dublin in October, to help publicize an Amnesty International campaign in support of the Universal Declaration of Human Rights. U2 signed this petition, and Bono spoke to the crowd: "One of the greatest problems in the world is the cynical idea that the world can't be changed and that politics and economics are too complicated to deal with. But with Amnesty it's simple; you can write a postcard and make a gigantic difference to the life of someone who is in jail or suffering human rights abuses."[4]

The next month, it was back to music—U2 released its first retrospective album, *U2 The Best of 1980–1990,* on November 2, 1998. It sped to the top of the charts around the world. While Bono and the band worked hard promoting the album, Bono was also working feverishly on behalf of an organization called Jubilee 2000.

He had originally been approached by them in 1997. Jubilee 2000 was an international coalition of organizations in more than forty countries. Their goal was the cancellation of debt for third-world countries, a debt that was making it impossible for those countries to pull themselves out of poverty. Its founder, Jamie Drummond, had learned that ten years after receiving the tremendous contributions raised by the Live Aid concert, Ethiopia had to spend twice that much *every year* to pay old debts to Western nations. Drummond wanted the music community to help again, and he contacted a lawyer at Island Records, U2's label. The lawyer put him in touch with Bono, who listened and signed on.[5]

He started by contacting Eunice Shriver, a member of the Kennedy family who was one of the founders of the Special Olympics. The powerful Kennedy clan had a long tradition of family members involved in public service and politics, including President

John F. Kennedy and Senators Robert and Edward Kennedy. He asked for her advice on how to go about reaching people in power, and she sent him to her son, Bobby. Bobby started by putting him in touch with a variety of politicians. He also sent Bono to a Harvard University professor, Jeffrey Sachs, so he could learn about the world of high finance and economics. "He turned the math into music," said Bono. Then Bono sought out economists whose views differed from Sachs's views; he needed to hear all sides of the story if he was to have answers for his critics.[6]

In June 1999, Bono and the Edge went to Cologne, Germany, along with thirty-five thousand other people who came to demonstrate in support of debt relief for poor nations. The leaders of the G-8—Canada, France, Germany, Italy, Japan, Russia, the United Kingdom, and the United States—were having a summit meeting there to discuss economic issues. Bono and Thom Yorke, a member of the band Radiohead, met publicly with German Chancellor Gerhard Schroeder and gave him a petition signed by twenty million people. The response was an announcement that a "Cologne Debt Initiative" was being formed, and that it would provide seventy billion dollars' worth of debt relief.[7] It was an outstanding beginning, but just the beginning.

The next step for Bono was participation in another all-star fundraising concert, NetAid, on October 9,

1999. It was actually composed of three concerts taking place simultaneously in the United States, England, and Switzerland, and was being broadcast live via the Internet in addition to being shown on MTV and VH1. The webcast reached 132 nations, and enabled NetAid to grant $1.7 million to fifteen organizations in Africa and Kosovo.[8] Bono and Haitian hip-hop artist Wyclef Jean performed a song they had recorded for NetAid, "New Day," and were accompanied by famed American music producer and

(left to right) Bono, Britain's Prime Minister Tony Blair, and concert organizer and musician Bob Geldof, at 1999's G-8 Summit in Cologne, Germany.

composer Quincy Jones and a thirty-piece orchestra. They had already played the song at a September benefit for the Wyclef Jean Foundation, which provides musical therapy, instruments, and lessons for underprivileged children around the world, as well as performing it at the United Nations.[9]

In between the trip to Cologne and the NetAid concert, Bono had more personal business to attend to. In August 1999, his first son, Elijah, was born.

In the course of working for the Jubilee 2000 Drop the Debt campaign, Bono took his case to President Bill Clinton, the United States Congress, and the United Nations. He met with Pope John Paul II at the Vatican, where the Pontiff tried on Bono's trademark sunglasses before giving a speech addressing the "inhumanity and injustice of poor countries spending so much of their national income paying back old loans to rich countries."[10]

Bono and Bobby Shriver went on to form a separate charitable organization, DATA. The name is an acronym for Debt, AIDS, and Trade for Africa. Their goal is to "raise awareness about, and spark response to the crises swamping Africa: unpayable Debts, uncontrolled spread of AIDS, and unfair Trade rules which keep Africans poor."[11]

Bono's charitable work, including his efforts on behalf of Jubilee 2000, earned him the 1999 MTV Free Your Mind award, which he received at the

MTV Europe Awards ceremony held in Dublin on November 11.

Somehow Bono also found the time to participate in two films in 1999, one of which he cowrote. He was briefly onscreen in director Phil Joanou's film *Entropy*; the role was what is called a "cameo" and his name did not appear in the film's credits. Bono then teamed up with writer Nicholas Klein to create the script for another Wim Wenders film, *The Million Dollar Hotel*. He composed and performed music for it, and was onscreen for another short appearance.[12]

Bono celebrated New Year's Eve of 1999 by attending "America's Millennium Gala" in Washington, D.C. He was invited by Quincy Jones, who had also given his support to Jubilee 2000 and was a coproducer of the gala. Bono performed the song "One," backed up by Daniel Lanois on guitar, plus a full orchestra. Before the show, though, Bono and his family greeted President Clinton and his family. It was an exciting ending to an exhausting year.

14

GLOBAL HUMANITARIAN

I feel like I've been wearing a bowler hat and carrying a briefcase," said Bono. "Now I have found my voice again and it's an amazing feeling."[1]

"Finding his voice" had more than one meaning for Bono. After countless hours spent working for Jubilee 2000, even without a bowler (a black hat traditionally worn by serious British businessmen) or briefcase, he was back to making music. U2 was in the studio, hard at work on their new album project. He was "finding his voice" as a songwriter, and the band had decided that after an entire decade of musical experimentation, they were ready to get back to basics, returning to the sound that had first established U2 as stars. Last but far from least, he felt he was singing better than he had in years, following a period of serious worries.

"I was having a lot of difficulty on the last tour. Everyone was saying it was my lifestyle, on the phone all the time, never going to bed, smoking, drinking too much, so I was making changes but I was just not able to really get there." Finally, he altered his diet, cut down his drinking, and quit smoking. It worked. "There are notes [on the new record] I haven't sung for years and years."[2]

While the band was home in Ireland, they were honored by the mayor of Dublin, who conferred "the Freedom of the City" on them and manager Paul

(left to right) Nigerian President Olusegun Obasanjo, United Nations Secretary-General Kofi Annan, and Bono at the United Nations Millennium Summit in 2000.

McGuinness during St. Patrick's Day festivities. "The Honorary Freedom of the City of Dublin is the highest honor the City can award to a person. It is awarded to those who achieve great levels in their field."[3] Among other things, this gave them an ancient privilege of being a "freeman," the right to graze sheep on public land—which Bono and the Edge proceeded to do! They both appeared the next day at Dublin's St. Stephen's Green carrying a lamb. Bono commented, "They are a lot easier to handle than pop stars." His lamb then made something of a mess on the sleeve of his leather jacket, which did not seem to upset him particularly. He said it reminded him of his band. In the next day's *Irish Times,* the band was renamed Ewe2.[4]

Even while the new album was in production, Bono kept traveling to support the cause of reducing Third World debt. He spoke at the United Nations Millennium Summit on September 7, 2000. Nigerian President Obasanjo, Ann Pettifor of Jubilee 2000, and Bono then gave Secretary-General Kofi Annan a Jubilee 2000 debt-relief petition bearing 21.2 million signatures gathered in more than 155 countries.[5]

He also visited congressmen in Washington. "In between the building of hospitals and schools and the commitment to cancel a hundred billion dollars in debt is a lot of red tape and bureaucracy . . . everyone passing the buck and people hiding in the small print. And we're going after each one of them."[6]

All That You Can't Leave Behind was released in late October 2000, and it became the band's most successful release since *The Joshua Tree*.[7] It debuted in the No. 1 spot in thirty-two countries,[8] and received praise from critics around the world. *Rolling Stone* called it U2's "third masterpiece."[9]

One country, however, was not as welcoming as the rest. Burma banned the record because it included "Walk On," a song dedicated to a political activist named Aung San Suu Kyi, who was then under house arrest.

Even when Bono was not in Washington himself, his efforts there made the news. When President Clinton signed a global debt relief measure on November 6, he made a point of praising Pope John Paul II and Bono. "When we get the pope and the pop stars all singing on the same sheet of music, our voices do carry to the heavens," said Clinton. He also said that Bono's "passionate devotion" to debt relief had brought together people from opposite ends of the political spectrum, from the very conservative Republican Senator Jesse Helms to Clinton's treasury secretary, Lawrence Summers.[10]

Clinton was fond of telling the story of Bono's first meeting with Summers. "Secretary Summers comes in to my office and says, 'You know, some guy just came in to see me in jeans and a T-shirt, and he just had one name, but he sure was smart. Do you know anything about him?'"[11]

Bono was not able to attend the signing ceremony, but there was a celebration he was not about to miss one week later: a surprise seventy-fifth birthday party for his father, Bob Hewson.

The party was held in Dublin at the Clarence Hotel, which Bono owned. All the lampposts on a nearby dock sported posters showing Bob, with the title "Still rocking at 75." And rock he did, with friends and family. According to The *Dubliner*, "[Bob] had been led to believe they were going for a quiet family meal. But the karaoke themed party was more pop than rock when the singing began. The hotel was adorned with giant posters proclaiming 'Bob Lives . . . just about. Still above ground, 75, Dublin, 13 November, 2000.'"[12] According to a friend of his, Bono was supposed to be at another party that night, "but as soon as this came along himself and Ali canceled. Bono is very close to his father and the truth is he loves karaoke."[13] Whatever would his fans say to that?!

The month of November ended with yet another celebration. This time, it was the premiere of the movie *The Million Dollar Hotel*, directed by Wim Wenders and starring Mel Gibson. Bono appears in the movie very briefly. He cowrote the screenplay with Nicholas

Klein, based on a story of Bono's, and U2 provided three songs for the soundtrack. One of the songs had lyrics written by internationally respected author Salman Rushdie. "Salman was writing a book about a rock band from India and he'd written lyrics for this imaginary rock band and he'd asked me to put music to them. So I did and U2 recorded the song, called 'The Ground Beneath Your Feet,' which is this kind of eternal love song and it was perfect for the end of the film, according to Wim."[14] The song was also included on *All That You Can't Leave Behind.*

December was miraculously quiet in comparison to the rest of the year, which was just as well. U2 was about to go touring again.

15

ELEVATION AND DEVASTATION

The new year certainly started well for U2. They had released the song "Beautiful Day" before the rest of *All That You Can't Leave Behind*, and it was a huge hit for them. On February 21, 2001, it earned them three Grammy Awards, for Record of the Year, Song of the Year, and Best Rock Performance by a Duo or Group. Then they had an appointment at the 2001 Brit Awards, on February 26. There, they received an award for "Outstanding Contribution to Music." They were the first non-British band to get this award, and it was not their only prize of the night. They also won the Best International Group award. Bono thanked the audience for their patience, adding, "We've been in a few odd places over the years. Bless you." U2 performed a song at the end of the show, and Bono waded out into the crowd, just as he had done so many times before.[1] It was a perfect warm-up for the series of concerts they had ahead. The tour was dubbed Elevation, which was the name of a song on *All That You Can't Leave Behind.* One of the song's lyrics was especially appropriate: "The goal is elevation."

This was not just another rock 'n' roll band on tour, after all. While it is common nowadays for celebrities to travel with large entourages, the groups of people that came along for this ride were a touch different. Volunteers from Greenpeace, Amnesty International, and Drop the Debt were at the shows, handing out their literature, talking up a storm, and selling T-shirts to raise funds.[2] The band did not have to preach from the stage; the messages were out in the lobby, waiting. The stage itself was simple and stripped down, a far cry from the enormous props and sets they had hauled along on the Zooropa and PopMart tours.

The band played in North America from March to June, in Europe from July to August, and returned to North America to finish the tour in October and November.

Ali was home in Ireland, pregnant with their fourth child. Bono called her from the stage every night to check on her. He ended each call by singing "All I Want Is You," a song from *Rattle and Hum.* He had to leave the tour in a hurry to make it home in

Harvard is not the only university to make Bono an honorary member of its graduating class. In 2004, Bono received an honorary Doctor of Laws degree from the University of Pennsylvania and also gave the commencement speech.

time for the arrival of their fourth child, John Abraham, in May.[3]

While he was in the States in June, Bono was invited to give a commencement address at Harvard University and was made an honorary member of the graduating class.[4]

Bono's father, Bobby, had cancer, and when the band returned to Europe for the middle segment of the tour, Bono visited him as often as he could. He often spoke about him onstage, telling the audience about him, and one night he introduced the song "Kite" by saying, "This is for my dad, Bob Hewson. He's only got a few days left in him." Nine days later, on August 21, Bono was with his father when he died. Although he was grieving deeply, Bono chose to continue with the tour, even performing that night rather than disappoint the seventeen thousand fans waiting to hear him.

Bono and the Edge played a new song together at his father's funeral, one Bono said he had composed especially for his father.[5] It was titled "Sometimes You Can't Make It On Your Own," and three years later it would be included on *How to Dismantle an Atomic Bomb*. The lyrics were, and are, heartbreaking. "And it's you when I look in the mirror / And it's you that makes it hard to let go / Sometimes you can't make it on your own."

Bono and bandmate Larry Mullen (behind Bono) help carry Bob
Hewson's coffin during the funeral which took place in Howth,
Ireland, on August 24, 2001.

He did go on, though, finishing the tour he had committed to months before.

Everything came to a halt on September 11, 2001. After the terrorist attacks that stunned the world, the band questioned whether they should play the remaining dates. They finally decided to go ahead, but first they took part in *America: A Tribute to Heroes*, a television program made to help the survivors and families of the victims. The attack on New York had extra significance for Bono, who had bought a luxury penthouse apartment on Central Park West that year.

U2 was scheduled to play in New York City in October, at Madison Square Garden. While other groups canceled New York shows, U2 showed up and did three nights at the Garden. As the song "Walk On" was playing, the names of the missing and dead in the attacks were displayed on a screen at the back of the stage.[6]

When U2 performed during halftime at Super Bowl XXXVI on February 3, 2002, they used a giant screen and again showed the names of the 9/11 dead, as Bono held an American flag. He said later, "It was like taking a big bite out of a giant apple pie. To feel the full embrace of America was the pinnacle."[7]

Just two days earlier, he had been on an altogether different kind of stage in Manhattan. It was the World Economic Forum, and Bono was on panels with South African Archbishop Desmond Tutu and U.S. Treasury

Secretary Paul O'Neill.[8] A month after the Super Bowl, Bono met with President George W. Bush at the White House. He was widely criticized for his willingness to meet with Bush, many of whose policies were tremendously unpopular with much of his audience. Even the Edge was uneasy about it. "He's done incredible work with the debt cancellation and the AIDS problem in Africa, but we wince sometimes when we see him with politicians in the newspaper. It's worth it, but

Bono sits alongside Senator Barack Obama at the National Prayer Breakfast in Washington, D.C. on February 2, 2006.

sometimes you realize how some people are [being critical]. Intellectually, we don't do these things thinking it's hip. We do it despite the fact that it's really unhip."[9]

Bono was aware of the reactions, and said, "I'd have lunch with Satan if so much was at stake. . . . So the band might cringe, I might wince, but I went to Washington to get a check and [later] I'm going back to get a bigger one."[10] He also met with National Security Advisor Condoleeza Rice, and spoke to her about increasing funds that rich nations offer to help poorer nations.[11]

Then it was back to business. Music business. On February 27, 2002, the annual Grammy Awards ceremonies were held at the Staples Center in Los Angeles. U2 performed and eventually went home with another four awards: Record of the Year, Best Pop Performance by a Duo or Group with Vocal, Best Rock Vocal Performance by a Duo or Group, and Best Rock Album.

It had been a good couple of months for awards—U2 had won an American Music Award for Internet Artist of the Year in January, and on February 15, Bono was given the Heart of Entertainment Award by the Entertainment Industry Foundation for "his extraordinary philanthropy and dedication to improving the lives of millions of people throughout the world."[12]

The March 4 issue of *Time* magazine had Bono on

its cover, and the majority of the story inside dealt with his charitable work rather than music. When he was singled out as one of "The 50 Most Powerful People in Music" by *Q Magazine* that year, the same thing happened. *Irish America* featured Bono and Ali in their August/September issue, and the writer focused on their work in Africa, and on Ali's activism on behalf of the Chernobyl Children's Project.

U2's fans were getting into the act, too. They had been listening to Bono talking as well as singing, and the U.S. Treasury Department received twenty *thousand* e-mails from them, urging action on debt relief. That may have played a role in convincing Treasury Secretary Paul O'Neill to accompany Bono on a tour of Africa. O'Neill had first thought that Bono was "just another celebrity who wanted to use me." But a meeting with Bono, and those e-mails, changed his mind.[13]

The press called them the odd couple, and it must have been quite a sight—the businessman and the rock star. They toured Ghana, South Africa, Uganda, and Ethiopia for eleven days. They met with everyone from heads of state to young mothers suffering from HIV, unable to afford the medicine that could save them. Although O'Neill was concerned about past waste of aid money, he was moved by what he saw and learned of the desperate conditions across the continent. Speaking at Georgetown University the next month, he said that he did not have specific recommendations yet, but that ". . . in the right environment focused on growth, enterprise, and human development, aid works. Knowing that it can work, we have a moral imperative to demand as much."[14]

As Bono traveled the globe on his mission for debt relief and more, another U2 record was being assembled. Released in November, it was their second "best of" collection, covering the years 1990 to 2000. Two new songs were added as a bonus. One of them, "The Hands That Built America," was used as the theme to the Martin Scorsese film *Gangs of New York*. It won a Golden Globe Award in January 2003 for Best Original Song and was also nominated for an Oscar in 2003. Bono had seen Scorsese years before, when he attended a master class on film directing that Scorsese gave in April 1999 at the Ardmore Studios outside Dublin.[15] The other bonus song, "Electrical Storm," was released ahead of the album and was already on the radio charts in October. In October 2002, the Irish postal service issued a gold stamp showing the entire band as part of their Irish Rock Legends stamp set.[16]

The legends, in the meantime, were heading for the recording studio once again.

16

AWARDS AND AN
ATOMIC BOMB

Nominations for the Nobel Peace Prize are announced in February each year. Four months after learning that Jimmy Carter had won in 2002, Bono learned on February 18, 2003, that he had been nominated for the second year in a row.

It was not the only honor he received that month. On February 21, Bono was given the MusiCares Foundation Person of the Year award at a gala celebration in New York City. The MusiCares Foundation was established in 1989 by The National Academy of Recording Arts and Sciences to provide a safety net for music people in times of need. The ceremony took place during Grammy Awards week, and consisted of a dinner and concert, with many speeches and wall-to-wall celebrities.

A tribute magazine filled with letters of praise was

printed for the guests, and its contributors included President Bill Clinton, Senator Hillary Clinton, and United Nations Secretary-General Kofi Annan. President Clinton wrote, "By shining an international spotlight on debt, poverty, and AIDS in Africa, and devoting your own energy and resources to address these issues, you have helped to create a brighter future for people throughout the continent—and you have given us all a powerful example of building personal success and a better world at the same time."[1]

One week later, on February 28, Bono was given the Chevalier of Legion of Honor by French President Jacques Chirac, in Paris. Next, on March 3, the Irish Music Awards gave him their Humanitarian Award, and U2 won their Best Group Award. Two weeks after that, the American Ireland Fund gave Bono their Humanitarian Award.

He had to wait until April 28 for his next honor, inclusion in the "European Heroes" issue of *Time* magazine's European edition. Another month passed, and U2 collected the Outstanding Song Collection award at the Novello Songwriting Awards in London. The run of awards ended on October 12, when "The Hands That Built America" won the Best Original Song prize at the World Soundtrack Awards in Belgium.

Bono went to Cape Town, South Africa, in November to perform at a charity fundraiser. It was

R&B singer Beyoncé Knowles and Bono visit the Baphumele children's home while in Cape Town, South Africa, for Nelson Mandela's 46664 Concert in 200

hosted by Nelson Mandela and was called the 46664 Concert—that was the number tattooed on Mandela during his thirty years as a political prisoner in South Africa. The concert organizers hoped to raise awareness of the global threat of HIV/AIDS, and to raise funds for the Nelson Mandela Foundation. Star performers came from around the world, and the concert was recorded and eventually released as three CDs.[2]

On January 17, 2004, Bono was back onstage—receiving yet another award, this time at the King

Center in Atlanta, Georgia. Coretta Scott King presented the award, praising Bono for his work with the AIDS crisis in Africa, Third World debt relief, and other issues, all in the spirit of her late husband, Martin Luther King, Jr. Bono spoke about how much Dr. King had inspired him and mentioned the two songs from *The Unforgettable Fire* that were dedicated to the civil rights leader, "MLK" and "Pride (In the Name of Love)."

Then it was time for music once more. U2 was recording their next album, which was scheduled to be released later that year. Bono was also, as the *Wall Street Journal* put it, "starting a new gig: media and entertainment investing."[3] He joined Elevation Partners, a fund that invested in a variety of entertainment companies. (The fund's name had nothing to do with the U2 song; it was just a coincidence!) It was a time of rapid change, as new technology made it possible to distribute music and film in new ways.

In fact, U2 was involved in one of the best-known developments in music distribution: the Apple iPod. The band worked out a deal with Apple, which was releasing a new version of the iPod dubbed the iPod U2 Special Edition. It came loaded with U2 songs, and U2 appeared in a television commercial for it. The first single from the new album was made available for downloading exclusively via iTunes, where it promptly became the biggest seller in the entire catalog.[4]

Bono continued his balancing act between family, music, and charity work. On September 23, he was one of one hundred recipients of Chile's highest award, the Pablo Neruda International Presidential Medal of Honour.[5] He was given the actual medal by Chile's ambassador to Ireland, in Dublin.

Finally, in November, the long-awaited new U2 album was released. Titled *How to Dismantle an Atomic Bomb*, it was a tremendous success, rising to the No. 1 position on the charts in over thirty countries.[6]

For Bono, it was a particularly important album. Before the album's release, he told a reporter that as he worked on the lyrics, he also came to terms with the death of his father in 2001:

> *Maybe something just lifted, like a very strange weight, and I am more at ease with myself. . . . He is the atomic bomb in question and it is his era, the cold-war era, and we had a bit of a cold war, myself and him. When he died, I had no idea what would happen. . . . I didn't know that grief affects you in surprising ways. I didn't know that two years later, when you're walking down the street, there's tears going down your face and you don't know why.[7]*

He said more about his relationship with his father a year later, when *Rolling Stone* featured him on their cover and printed a lengthy interview with him. "By not encouraging me to be a musician, even though that's all he ever wanted to be, he's made me one. By telling me never to have big dreams or else, that to dream is to be disappointed, he made me have big dreams. By telling me that the band would only last five minutes or ten minutes—we're still here. . . . I loved my dad. But we were combatants."[8]

When Oprah Winfrey interviewed Bono before *How to Dismantle an Atomic Bomb* came out, she asked him, "Do you have anxiety every time you release an album?" He said yes, adding, "It's much easier to be successful than it is to be relevant. The tricks won't keep you relevant. Tricks might keep you popular for a while, but in all honesty, I don't know how U2 will stay relevant. I know we've got a future. I know we can fill stadiums. And yet, with every record, I think, *Is this it? Are we still relevant?*"[9]

After the album's release, Bono said simply, "It's just such a personal record. It may just be our best."[10]

17

"THE CONSTANT CHARMER"

"I'm sick of Bono. And I am Bono. It's like, oh, man, shut up. But there it is. You just don't want to be dull. We might be annoying. But we're not dull."

Bono was answering a question about being worried about preaching onstage. He added, "I'm scared of embarrassing my bandmates and our audience, but I am [convinced] that this is a generation that wants to be remembered for something other than the war against terror or the Internet."[1]

U2, in the meantime, was making sure it would be remembered for the sheer quantity of Grammy awards it received. On February 13, the band picked up two more Grammys, for Best Rock Performance by a Duo or Group with Vocal, and for Best Rock Song. The video for

"Vertigo" won the award for Best Short Form Music Video.

It was another gala night for the band. Bono made headlines for himself five days later, when he was nominated for the Nobel Peace Prize for the second time. He was also in the press courtesy of the *Los Angeles Times*, which ran an editorial on February 25 urging that Bono be nominated for the position of president of the World Bank. The World Bank is an organization whose purpose is to lend money and give technical help to aid economic development in poor countries.

When the treasury secretary, John Snow, was questioned about the possibility, he did not dismiss it altogether, saying, "He's somebody I admire. He does a lot of good in this world of economic development."[2]

Bono did not get the job, which was just as well—he was due to start the Vertigo tour. Overdue, in fact. The tour was delayed for a month due to illness in the family of one of U2's members. The band never gave the details to the press, as it was a private matter, and they hit the road at the end of March 2005, beginning a five-part tour that ended in Hawaii on December 16, 2006.

Of course, music was not the only item on Bono's plate as the band circled the globe. In the spring of 2005, he and his wife Ali joined forces with designer Rogan Gregory to start the EDUN fashion line.

Ali prefers to stay in the background, but she gets quite a bit done there. She has been very active in her support of the Chernobyl Children's Project, which was formed to help the victims of fallout from the disaster at the Russian nuclear plant in Chernobyl in 1986. In 1995, she helped to produce an award-winning documentary, *Black Wind, White Land—Living with Chernobyl*. She also narrated *Chernobyl Heart*, which won an Oscar in 2004. In addition, Ali was active in the movement to shut down Sellafield, a

U2 performs on the Vertigo tour which lasts more than a year and a half.

British nuclear plant across the Irish Sea from their home in Ireland. Generally, Ali avoided the headlines but not the issues behind them.

EDUN combines high fashion with high ideals. "EDUN is utilizing locally-run factories in Africa, South Africa, and India. These facilities have all been personally inspected and approved by the EDUN team, ensuring that they operate on sound business

ono, his wife Alison Stewart, and designer Rogan Gregory arrive at the EDUN lothing line launch party taking place at the Saks Fifth Avenue store in Beverly lills, California.

and ethical bases."[3] The partners hope that other companies will want to copy their work, and see that it is possible to do business in an ethical way and still make a profit. So far, they have placed their clothing in stores in six countries, and it is available everywhere through the Internet.

Between March 2005 and December 2006, it seemed that U2 was everywhere, too. They played in North and South America, Europe, Australia, and Japan. The tour was divided into five segments with breaks built in. While they were playing in Europe, Bono joined with Bob Geldof and many others to organize yet another mega-concert, Live 8.

Live 8 was a series of ten concerts that took place around the world on July 2, 2005. One hundred and fifty bands, containing 1,250 musicians, were watched by an estimated 3 billion people. Unlike other similar concerts, such as Live Aid, Live 8 was not a fundraiser. Instead, they asked people to send in their names to be put on a petition for debt relief. They ultimately got more than 30 million names, and the list was presented to G-8 chairman Tony Blair. The G-8, the political leaders of the eight richest countries in the world, were having a summit meeting in Scotland on July 6.

By the time the summit was over, the G-8 leaders had made remarkable promises regarding debt relief and more. They committed to $50 billion more aid per year by 2010, providing AIDS drugs to those in need, debt cancellation for thirty-eight countries, and free education and healthcare for children—it was quite a list. As of early 2007, however, they had yet to follow through on all their promises.[4]

A few weeks after Live 8, U2 closed the European tour with a stop in Portugal, where they received the country's Order of Liberty award in honor of their ongoing humanitarian work on August 14, 2005.

The band toured North America from September 9 through December 19. During that stretch, Bono appeared on the covers of *Rolling Stone* and *The New York Times Magazine.*[5] One week after the tour ended, he saw himself on one last cover for the year. It was *Time* magazine, and he was standing with Bill and Melinda Gates. They had been named Persons of the Year.

The articles that accompanied the cover are filled with the details of the extraordinary work done by all three of them, and praise for that work. The piece that focuses on Bono alone is called "The Constant Charmer," and the subtitle did its job by summing up the article perfectly: "The inside story of how the world's biggest rock star mastered the political game and persuaded the world's leaders to take on global poverty. And he's not done yet."[6]

What the writer did not say, and probably did not know, was that there were times when the band was almost done with Bono. "When I do my rant on making poverty history, I have got Larry Mullen, our drummer, behind me looking at his watch, timing me. . . . There was one point when I thought, 'I'm going to be thrown out of the band for this stuff."[7]

A Gap store in San Francisco, California, displays Product RED merchandise, of which half the profits will be used to help people affected with HIV/AIDS.

Usually, stories about rock 'n' roll bands appear only in the music press or gossip columns. It is a measure of U2's standing that Bono's comments were reported by the Associated Press, and the story ran in newspapers around the world.

When all was said and done, though, the four friends supported one another, as they had for almost thirty years.

Bono found himself back on another magazine cover the very next month, when the British *Q Magazine* declared him to be The Man of the Year in January 2006.[8] On January 26, the man of the year started the year by joining forces with his old friend Bobby Shriver to announce the formation of Product RED. They teamed up with a handful of enormous corporations that agreed to donate part of the profits made on items that would be marketed as Product RED pieces. American Express offered a RED card, Converse sneakers developed a RED collection of sneakers made of African mudcloth, the Gap chose a T-shirt made in Africa, and the list is growing. The money is used to support a variety of programs that help women and children who are affected by HIV/AIDS in Africa.[9]

The next stop for Bono was Washington, D.C., to address the National Prayer Breakfast. President and Mrs. Bush were there, as well as members of Congress, the Cabinet, the military, the clergy, and countries from around the world. Bono had put white plastic bracelets from The ONE Campaign to fight AIDS and poverty at each table. The breakfast was held in a ballroom at the Hilton Washington Hotel, and Bono set his listeners at ease instantly, starting his remarks by saying, "Please join me in praying that I don't say something we'll all regret."

He went on to talk about the place of religion in his life, and the need for people of all faiths to band together to fight AIDS and poverty, pointing out in passing that the Scriptures he had studied so closely had no less than twenty-one hundred references to poverty. He praised the leaders for the progress they had made, and insisted that more be done. Bono quoted Scriptures from Christianity, Judaism, and Islam to make his points, and asked that America give 1 percent of the federal budget to the poor.[10]

Bono spent the next weekend with U2, collecting four Grammy Awards in Los Angeles. The band won Album of the Year, Song of the Year, Best Rock Performance by a Duo or Group with Vocal, and Best Rock Song. When he accepted the award for Song of the Year, Bono said that much of the album was about his difficult relationship with his father: "He was the atomic bomb in question."[11]

The band had to take their celebration on the road; the tour had started up again. They swung through South America this time, and while they were in São Paolo, Brazil, Bono met with Brazilian president Luiz Inacio Lula da Silva and Minister of Culture Gilberto Gil, who had been a famous musician before joining the government. Bono and Lula had met in Davos at the World Economic Summit in 2005. Lula had started a poverty program called Zero Hunger, and Bono said he planned to donate the guitar he used in the São Paolo concerts to the program.[12]

The tour moved on to Chile, where Chilean president Ricardo Lagos gave Bono the Neruda Prize, Chile's highest award for the arts, on February 26. In a strange twist of fate, one week after Bono gave his guitar away in Brazil, Lagos gave Bono a traditional Andean instrument called a charango, which looks like a small lute. Lagos said, "When we were talking before, Bono told me that one must study throughout one's life. So for his next concert here, I hope he's learned how to play the charango."[13]

It was a week for awards. Before the band played that night, they received Amnesty International's 2005 Ambassador of Conscience award. Manager Paul McGuinness was also a recipient.[14] And two days earlier, Bono had been nominated for the Nobel Peace Prize; for the third time. His longtime friend and fellow activist, Bob Geldof, was also nominated.

In November, Bono and Geldof gave their support to a program dedicated to raising money to buy vaccines for children in developing countries. The goal is to "immunize 500 million children by 2015, saving ten million lives, and help eradicate polio from the world," according to then British finance minister Gordon Brown.[15] Brown later became the United Kingdom's prime minister in June 2007.

And so the year went, as had so many before. The band toured, Bono worked hard on behalf of many worthy causes, and spent as much time as he could with his family, calling them regularly from the road. U2 is planning yet another album, and twenty-seven years after answering that open call for people looking to start a band, Bono is enjoying himself.

"I used to think that one day I'd be able to resolve the different drives I have in different directions, the tension between the different people I am. Now I realize that is who I am, and I'm more content to be discontent. I do feel I'm getting closer to the song I hear in my head, getting closer to not compromising that melody . . ."

"I wasn't looking for grace, but luckily grace was looking for me."[16]

CHRONOLOGY

May 10: Paul David Hewson (Bono) is born.   **1960**

September: Enters Mount Temple High   **1972**
School, where he will meet future U2 bandmates.

September 10: Mother, Iris, dies.   **1974**

Larry Mullen posts a note at school, looking   **1976**
for people interested in forming a band; Bono
responds and joins the band.

Band settles on the name U2; May 25:   **1978**
Paul McGuinness meets the band and agrees to
become their manager.

U2 signs first major record deal, with   **1979**
Island Records.

August 21: Bono marries Alison Stewart.   **1982**

June 5: Red Rocks concert takes place in   **1983**
Denver, Colorado; later chosen as one of the
"50 Moments That Changed the History of Rock
and Roll" by *Rolling Stone* magazine.

March 14: U2 dubbed "The Band of the   **1985**
'80s" by *Rolling Stone* magazine; July 13:
Performs at Live Aid concert.

May: Daughter, Jordan, is born.   **1989**

1991	July: Daughter, Memphis Eve, is born.
1999	August: Son, Elijah Bob Patricious Guggi Q., is born.
2001	May: Son, John Abraham, is born; August 21: Father, Bob Hewson, dies.
2005	July 2: Performs at Live 8 concert.
2006	December 23: Awarded an honorary British knighthood for his humanitarian work and his contributions to the music industry.
2007	Appears in major motion picture release, *Across the Universe*; September 27: Is given the prestigious Liberty Medal in Philadelphia, Pennsylvania, in recognition of his work with DATA. Past winners of the medal include Nelson Mandela and former presidents Carter, George H. W. Bush, and Clinton.

CHAPTER NOTES

Chapter 1. A Love Beyond Faith

1. U2 and Neil McCormick, *U2 by U2* (New York: HarperCollins, 2006), p. 15.

2. Eamon Dunphy, *Unforgettable Fire: Past, Present, and Future—The Definitive Biography of U2* (New York: Warner Books, 1987), pp. 14–15; Mick *Wall, Bono: In the Name of Love* (New York: Thunder's Mouth Press, 2005), p. 22.

Chapter 2. A Conflicted Child

1. Eamon Dunphy, *Unforgettable Fire: Past, Present, and Future—The Definitive Biography of U2* (New York: Warner Books, 1987), p. 16.

2. Ibid, p. 17.

3. U2 and Neil McCormick, *U2 by U2* (New York: HarperCollins, 2006), p. 15.

4. Dunphy, p. 19.

5. Bill Flanagan, *U2 at the End of the World* (New York: Delacorte Press, 1995), p. 525; Mick Wall, *Bono: In the Name of Love* (New York: Thunder's Mouth Press, 2005), p. 24.

6. U2 and McCormick, p. 16.

7. Wall, p. 23; Dunphy, p. 23.

8. Michka Assayas, *Bono: In Conversation* (New York: Riverhead Books, 2005), p. 31.

9. Laura Jackson, *Bono: His Life, Music, and Passions* (New York: Citadel Press, 2001), p. 5.

10. Dunphy, pp. 21–22.

11. Wall, p. 23.

12. Assayas, pp. 20–21; Dunphy, p. 23.

13. Wall, p. 26.

Chapter 3. High School Heaven

1. Mick Wall, *Bono: In the Name of Love* (New York: Thunder's Mouth Press, 2005), p. 27.

2. Ibid.

3. Michka Assayas, *Bono: In Conversation* (New York: Riverhead Books, 2005), p. 12.

4. Eamon Dunphy, *Unforgettable Fire: Past, Present, and Future—The Definitive Biography of U2* (New York: Warner Books, 1987), p. 31.

5. Wall, p. 28.

6. Laura Jackson, *Bono: His Life, Music, and Passions* (New York: Citadel Press, 2001), p. 5.

7. Wall, p. 29.

Chapter 4. Tragedy Strikes

1. U2 and Neil McCormick, *U2 by U2* (New York: HarperCollins, 2006), p. 14.

2. Mick Wall, *Bono: In the Name of Love* (New York: Thunder's Mouth Press, 2005), p. 24.

3. David Breskin, "Bono: The *Rolling Stone* Interview," *Rolling Stone*, October 8, 1987.

4. Michka Assayas, *Bono: In Conversation* (New York: Riverhead Books, 2005), p. 12.

5. Wall, pp. 32–35.

6. Ibid, p. 39.

7. Christopher Connelly, "Keeping the Faith," *U2: The Rolling Stone Files* (New York: Rolling Stone Press, 1994), p. 32.

8. Wall, p. 38.

9. David Schaffer, *People in the News: Bono* (Farmington Hill, Mich.: Lucent Books, 2004), pp. 18–19.

10. Assayas, p. 12.

Chapter 5. A Rock Star Is Born

1. Jay Cocks, "Band on the Run," *Time*, Vol. 129, No. 17, April 27, 1987.

2. Laura Jackson, *Bono: His Life, Music, and Passions* (New York: Citadel Press, 2001), p. 9.

3. Anthony DeCurtis and James Henke, eds., *The* Rolling Stone *Illustrated History of Rock & Roll*, Third Edition (New York: Random House, 1992), p. 634.

4. Jackson, pp. 13–15.

Chapter 6. A "Baby Band" Takes Its First Steps

1. Eamon Dunphy, *Unforgettable Fire: Past, Present, and Future—The Definitive Biography of U2* (New York: Warner Books, 1987), pp. 113–115, 118.

2. James Henke, "Blessed Are the Peacemakers," *Rolling Stone*, Vol. 397, June 9, 1983.

3. Dunphy, pp. 119–120.

4. Ibid., p. 122.

5. Ibid., p. 128.

6. Matt McGee, "The History of U2–3," *@U2*, n.d., <http://www.atu2.com/collectors/columns/u23/> (July 2, 2007).

7. Dunphy, pp. 139–140.

8. Ibid., pp. 143–146.

Chapter 7. Success at Last

1. James Henke, Review of *Boy*, *Rolling Stone*, Vol. 337, February 19, 1981.

2. Jon Pareles, Review of *October*, *Rolling Stone*, Vol. 362, February 4, 1982.

3. "U2 Discography: *Boy*," *U2.com*, n.d., <http://www.u2.com/music/index.php?album_id=3&type=lp> (July 5, 2007).

4. Mick Wall, *Bono: In the Name of Love* (New York: Thunder's Mouth Press, 2005), p. 85.

5. Eamon Dunphy, *Unforgettable Fire: Past, Present, and Future—The Definitive Biography of U2* (New York: Warner Books, 1987), pp. 190–191.

6. U2 and Neil McCormick, *U2 by U2* (New York: HarperCollins, 2006), p. 116.

7. Wall, p. 90.

8. Dunphy, pp 196–197.

9. "U2 Discography: *War*," *U2.com*, n.d., <http://www.u2.com/music/index.php?album_id=4&type=lp> (July 5, 2007).

10. Adrian Thrill, "War and Peace," *NME Originals*, February 26, 1983.

11. Ibid.

12. Wall, p. 104.

13. Dunphy, p. 210.

14. Wall, p. 100.

Chapter 8. "The Band of the '80s"

1. Mick Wall, *Bono: In the Name of Love* (New York: Thunder's Mouth Press, 2005), p. 106.

2. "50 Moments That Changed the History of Rock and Roll," *Rolling Stone*, June 24, 2004, p. 146.

3. "U2 Discography: *Under A Blood Red Sky*," *U2.com*, n.d., <http://www.u2.com/music/index.php?album_id=5&type=lp> (July 5, 2007).

4. Eamon Dunphy, *Unforgettable Fire: Past, Present, and*

Future—The Definitive Biography of U2 (New York: Warner Books, 1987), p. 232.

5. Ibid., pp. 235–236.

6. "1984 Music Awards," *Rolling Stone*, Vol. 443, February 28, 1985, pp. 36–27.

7. *Fóruns da Ultraviolet*, October 26, 2005, <http://www.ultraviolet-u2.com/foruns/archive/index.php/t-3141.html> (October 1, 2007).

8. Christopher Connelly, "Keeping the Faith," *Rolling Stone*, Vol. 443, March 14, 1985, p.25.

Chapter 9. Reconciling Rock and Religion

1. Mick Wall, *Bono: In the Name of Love* (New York: Thunder's Mouth Press, 2005), p. 11, and *Bono: His Life, Music, and Passions*, p. 67.

2. Michka Assayas, *Bono: In Conversation* (New York: Riverhead Books, 2005), p. 211.

3. Wall, p. 12.

4. Graham Jones, "Live Aid 1985: A Day of Magic," *CNN.com*, July 6, 2005, <http://www.cnn.com/2005/SHOW BIZ/Music/07/01/liveaid.memories/index.html?iref=newssearch> (July 2, 2007).

5. Adrian Thrills, "Cactus World Views," *NME Originals*, March 14, 1987.

6. Assayas, p. 224.

7. Ibid., p. 222.

8. Anthony DeCurtis, "Truths and Consequences," *Rolling Stone*, Vol. 499, May 7, 1987.

9. David Schaffer, *People in the News: Bono* (Farmington Hill, Mich.: Lucent Books, 2004), p. 50.

10. "U2 Where the Streets Have No Name Single," U2Wanderer, 1995–2007, <http://www.u2wanderer. org/disco/sing020.html> (July 10, 2007); Also Eamon Dunphy, *Unforgettable Fire: Past, Present, and Future—The Definitive Biography of U2* (New York: Warner Books, 1987), pp. 261–262.

Chapter 10. "The Big One"

1. Steve Pond, Review of *The Joshua Tree*, *Rolling Stone*, Vol. 497, April 9, 1987.

2. Sean O'Hagan, "The Band of Holy Joy," *New Music Express (NME)*, June 6, 1987.

3. Mick Wall, *Bono: In the Name of Love* (New York: Thunder's Mouth Press, 2005), p. 148.

4. Michka Assayas, *Bono: In Conversation* (New York: Riverhead Books, 2005), p. 154.

5. David Breskin, "Bono: The *Rolling Stone* Interview," *Rolling Stone*, Vol. 510, October 8, 1987.

6. Ibid.

7. Ibid.

8. O'Hagan.

9. Ibid.

Chapter 11. Media Frenzy and Social Change

1. "Year-End Random Notes," *Rolling Stone*, December 15–29, 1988.

2. Jack Barron, Interview (no title), *New Music Express (NME)*, October 22, 1988, p. 28.

3. Sean O'Hagan, "The Gospel of Heaven and Hell," *New Music Express (NME)*, December 19/26, 1987, p. 10.

4. Barron.

5. Steve Pond, "Now What?" *Rolling Stone*, Vol. 547, March 9, 1989.

6. "U2 Biography," *Three Chords and the Truth*, n.d., <http://www.threechordsandthetruth.net/u2bios/> (July 6, 2007).

7. *Rolling Stone: 100 Greatest Albums of the Eighties*, Vol. 565, November 16, 1989.

8. Laura Jackson, *Bono: His Life, Music, and Passions* (New York: Citadel Press, 2001), p. 105.

9. David Schaffer, *People in the News: Bono* (Farmington Hill, Mich.: Lucent Books, 2004), pp. 63–64.

10. "U2 Discography: *Achtung Baby*," *U2.com*, n.d., <http://www.u2.com/music/index.php?album_ id=9&type=lp> (July 5, 2007).

11. *Rolling Stone/MTV* poll, quoted in Schaffer, p. 66.

Chapter 12. Life in a Zoo

1. "U2 Discography: *Achtung Baby*," *U2.com*, n.d., <http://www.u2.com/music/index.php?album_ id=9&type=lp> (July 5, 2007).

2. Bill Flanagan, *The* Rolling Stone *Illustrated History of Rock and Roll*, p. 638.

3. Michka Assayas, *Bono: In Conversation* (New York: Riverhead Books, 2005), pp. 38–39.

4. Kevin Byrne, "U2 Biography: Bono," *@U2.com*, n.d., <http://www.atu2.com/band/bono/> (July 5, 2007).

5. Mick Wall, *Bono: In the Name of Love* (New York: Thunder's Mouth Press, 2005), p. 177.

6. Ibid., p. 190.

7. John Waters, *Race of Angels: The Genesis of U2* (Trafalgar Square, 1996), quoted on *U2.com*.

8. "Bono: Biography," *Answers.com*, n.d., <http://www.answers.com/topic/bono?cat=entertainment> (July 9, 2007).

9. Wall, pp. 95–96.

10. Ibid., pp. 197–199.

11. Ibid., pp. 200–201.

12. Ibid., p. 203.

13. "Paul McGuinness on MSN," *U2Station.com*, September 22, 1997, <http://www.u2station.com/news/archives/1997/09/index.php> (July 2, 2007).

14. CNN staff, "U2 Brings Peace, Love, and Rock 'n' Roll to Sarajevo," *U2tours.com*, September 23, 1997, <http://www.u2tours.com/displaymedia.src?ID=19970923&XID=526&Return=> (July 9, 2007).

15. "Edge's Blog by Regina O'Numb," *U2.com*, March 21, 1998, <http://www.reginaonumb.blogger.com.br/2005_03_01_archive.html> (July 5, 2007).

Chapter 13. Working Toward a Better World

1. "U2's Bono Helps Promote Belfast Peace Agreement," *CNN Interactive*, May 19, 1998, <http://www.cnn.com/SHOWBIZ/Music/9805/19/u2/index.html> (July 9, 2007).

2. Michka Assayas, *Bono: In Conversation* (New York: Riverhead Books, 2005), pp. 172–173.

3. *Irish News*, August 27, 1997, quoted on *u2tours.com*.

4. "U2 Discography: *Boy*," *U2.com*, n.d., <http://www.u2.com/music/index.php?album_id=3&type=lp> (July 5, 2007).

5. Mick Wall, *Bono: In the Name of Love* (New York: Thunder's Mouth Press, 2005), p. 252–253.

6. Ibid.

7. Ibid., p. 254.

8. "NetAid History," *NetAid.org*, n.d., <http://www.netaid.org/about/history.html> (July 2, 2007).

9. Brian Hiatt, "Bono, Wyclef Bring Out the Stars for NetAid Benefit," *@U2.com*, October 11, 1999, <http://www.atu2.com/news/article.src?Cat=&ID=576&Key=&Year=1999> (July 9, 2007).

10. Assayas, p. 202.

11. "Aid Working in Africa, But G8 Countries Seriously Off Track in Meeting Promises, says DATA Report 2007," *DATA.org*, May 15, 2007, <http://www.data.org/news/press_200705 15.html> (July 2, 2007).

12. "Where Two Roads Meet—*The Million Dollar Hotel*, and *All That You Can't Leave Behind*," *U2faq.com*, n.d., <http://www.u2faqs.com/history/f.html> (July 9, 2007).

Chapter 14. Global Humanitarian

1. Paul Majendie, *Reuters/Variety*, October 28, 2000.

2. Neil McCormick, "Confessions of a Rock Star," *Hot Press*, December 15, 2000.

3. "Freedom of the City," *dublincity.ie*, n.d., <http://www.dublincity.ie/living_in_the_city/kidsplus/city_hall/freedom_of_the_city-_kids_guide.asp> (July 2, 2007).

4. Roisin Ingle, *Irish Times*, March 20, 2000.

5. "Bono Takes World-record-breaking Debt Petition to Millennium Summit," *NY Rock*, September 6, 2000, <www.nyrock.com> (July 2, 2007).

6. McCormick.

7. Mick Wall, *Bono: In the Name of Love* (New York: Thunder's Mouth Press, 2005), p. 276.

8. David Schaffer, *People in the News: Bono* (Farmington Hill, Mich.: Lucent Books, 2004), p. 85.

9. James Hunter, Review of *All That You Can't Leave Behind*, *Rolling Stone*, Vol. 853, November 9, 2000.

10. Randall Mikkelsen, "Clinton Signs Global Debt Relief Measure," *Reuters*, November 6, 2000.

11. Josh Tyrangiel, "Can Bono Save the World?" *Time*, March 4, 2002, <http://www.time.com/time/covers/110102 0304/story.html> (July 2, 2007).

12. *The Dubliner*, June 2005.

13. "Bono's Dad Still Rocking at 75," *ShowBiz Ireland*, November 13, 2000.

14. Helen Barlow, "Bono on a Wim and a Prayer," *Sun Herald*, Australia, November 19, 2000.

Chapter 15. Elevation and Devastation

1. Laura Jackson, *Bono: His Life, Music, and Passions* (New York: Citadel Press, 2001), pp. 214–215.

2. Mick Wall, *Bono: In the Name of Love* (New York: Thunder's Mouth Press, 2005), p. 286.

3. Ibid., p. 227.

4. Jackson, p. 212.

5. Wall, pp. 231–232.

6. David Schaffer, *People in the News: Bono* (Farmington Hill, Mich.: Lucent Books, 2004), p. 88.

7. Tom Gliatto et al., "Bono's World," *People*, March 4, 2002, p. 74.

8. Ibid.

9. Tom Doyle, "10 Years of Turmoil Inside U2," *Q Magazine*, October 10, 2002.

10. Wall, p. 256.

11. Joseph Kahn, "A Star Close to the Heart of Aid Policy," *The New York Times*, March 15, 2002, <http://query.nytimes. com/gst/fullpage.html?sec=health&res=9E05E3D81139F936A2 5750C0A9649C8B63> (July 2, 2007).

12. Dean Goodman, "Hollywood Hails U2's Bono for Philanthropy," *Reuters NewsMedia*, February 15, 2002, <http://www.aegis.com/news/re/2002/RE020220.html> (July 2, 2007).

13. Ibid.

14. "Odd Couple," *Online NewsHour*, Jim Lehrer transcript from June 5, 2002, story reported by Kwame Holman, <http://www.pbs.org/newshour/bb/africa/jan-june02/oddcouple_6-5.html> (July 2, 2007).

15. Jackson, p. 185.

16. "History FAQ," U2: *U2faqs.com*, 2002–2006, <http://www.u2faqs.com/history/g.html#5> (July 23, 2007).

Chapter 16. Awards and an Atomic Bomb

1. "Letter from President Bill Clinton," *MusiCares Tribute Journal*, 2003.

2. Mick Wall, *Bono: In the Name of Love* (New York: Thunder's Mouth Press, 2005), pp. 292–294.

3. Robert A. Guth, "Bono Brings Star Power to Silicon Valley Fund," *Wall Street Journal*, June 15, 2004, <http://www.aegis.com/news/wsj/2004/WJ040607.html> (July 2, 2007).

4. Wall, p. 304.

5. "John Ralston Saul Awarded the Pablo Neruda International Presidential Medal of Honour," Governor General of Canada Web site, September 23, 2004, <http://www.gg.ca/media/doc.asp?lang=e&DocID=4267> (July 2, 2007).

6. Wall, p. 305.

7. *The Sunday Times Magazine*, November 7, 2004.

8. Jann Wenner, "Bono: The *Rolling Stone* Interview," *Rolling Stone*, Vol., 986, November 3, 2005, p.51.

9. Oprah Winfrey, "Oprah Talks to Bono," *O: The Oprah Magazine*, April 2004, p. 198.

10. "U2 Discography: *How To Dismantle An Atomic Bomb*," *U2.com*, n.d., <http://www.u2.com/music/index.php?album_id=68&type=lp> (July 5, 2007).

Chapter 17. "The Constant Charmer"

1. Jann Wenner, "Bono: The *Rolling Stone* Interview," *Rolling Stone*, Vol., 986, November 3, 2005, p. 62.

2. "Could Bono Handle the Bank?," *CNNMoney.com*, March 9, 2005, <http://money.cnn.com/2005/03/07/news/newsmakers/bono_worldbank/> (July 9, 2007).

3. "Edun Apparel," *Zappos.com*, n.d., <http://www.zappos.com/n/br/b/1514.html> (July 9, 2007).

4. "Latest News," *Live 8*, <http://www.live8live.com/latestnews/> (July 9, 2007).

5. *Rolling Stone*, November 3, 2005, and *New York Times Magazine*, September 18, 2005.

6. Josh Tyrangiel, "The Constant Charmer," *Time*, December 26, 2005, p. 46.

7. Associated Press, December 31, 2005.

8. Michael Odell, "The Q Interview," *Q Magazine*, January 2006, p. 62.

9. "Bono Signs Big Names to Fight AIDS with Shopping," http://www.joinred.com. Also see *Reuters*, January 26, 2006, and *The Financial Times*, January 26, 2006, p. 1.

10. "Bono at National Prayer Breakfast—Full Remarks," *Hunger for Justice*, February 2, 2006, <http://hungerforjustice.net/post/bono-at-national-prayer-breakfast-full-remarks/> (July 9, 2007).

11. Jeff Leeds and Lorne Manly, "U2 Overshadows Mariah Carey's Comeback Story at the Grammys," *The New York Times*, February 9, 2006, p. A25.

12. Edla Lula, "In Brazil, Bono Calls Lula Something the World Never Saw," *Brazzil Magazine*, February 20, 2006.

13. "Bono Receives Chile's Neruda Prize," *Billboard.com*, February 27, 2006, <http://www.billboard.com/bbcom/news/article_display.jsp?vnu_content_id=1002075323> (July 9, 2007).

14. Ibid.

15. "Bond Offering Aims to Raise Vaccination Money for Poor Children," *CBC News*, November 7, 2006, <http://www.cbc.ca/health/story/2006/11/07/bonds.html> (July 7, 2007).

16. Wenner.

ᵃ86978996757

FURTHER READING

Books

Assayas, Michka. *Bono: In Conversation.* New York: Riverhead Books, 2005.

Bono, The Edge, Adam Clayton, Larry Mullen, Jr., with Neil McCormick. *U2 by U2.* New York: HarperCollins, 2006.

Dunphy, Eamon. *Unforgettable Fire: Past, Present, and Future—The Definitive Biography of U2.* New York: Warner Books, 1987.

Editors of *Rolling Stone. U2: The Ultimate Compendium of Interviews, Articles, Facts, and Opinions from the Files of* Rolling Stone. New York: Hyperion, 1994.

Jackson, Laura. *Bono: His Life, Music, and Passions.* New York: Citadel Press, 2001.

Schaffer, David. *People in the News: Bono.* Farmington Hill, Mich.: Lucent Books, 2004.

Wall, Mick. *Bono: In the Name of Love.* New York: Thunder's Mouth Press, 2005.

Internet Addresses

U2 Official Site
http://www.u2.com

U2 on Tour at U2tours.com
http://www.u2tours.com

U2 FAQs
http://www.u2faqs.com

INDEX

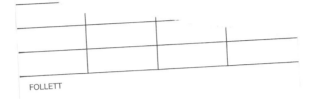

FOLLETT